THE HIST?RIAN'S CONSCIENCE

THE
HIST?RIAN'S
CONSCIENCE

Australian historians on the
ethics of history

Edited by
STUART MACINTYRE

MELBOURNE UNIVERSITY PRESS

MELBOURNE UNIVERSITY PRESS
an imprint of Melbourne University Publishing Ltd
PO Box 1167, Carlton, Victoria 3053, Australia
mup-info@unimelb.edu.au
www.mup.com.au

First published 2004

Typeset in Malaysia by Syarikat Seng Teik Sdn. Bhd.
Printed in Australia by McPherson's Printing Group
Designed by Phil Campbell

National Library of Australia Cataloguing-in-Publication entry

Macintyre, Stuart, 1947– .
    The historian's conscience: Australian historians on the ethics
    of history.
    Bibliography.
    Includes index.
    ISBN 0 522 85139 8.

    1. Historians—Australia. 2. History—Moral and ethical aspects.
    3. Historiography—Australia. I. Macintyre, Stuart, 1947– .
907.2094

To predict the Future, to manage the Present, would not be so impossible had not the Past been so sacrilegiously mishandled; effaced, and what is worse, defaced!

Carlyle, *Past and Present*, Book 4, Chapter 1.

CONTENTS

ACKNOWLEDGEMENTS

This book was conceived in a conversation with Louise Adler, the director of Melbourne University Publishing, and Sybil Nolan, the commissioning editor. We thought it would be helpful to move beyond the narrow and polemical terms of the History Wars by inviting a range of historians to explain how they deal with the ethical issues that arise from their work. Having convinced me to assemble such a collection, they then applied their considerable persuasive skills to the contributors. I write in the Introduction that 'we invited a number of historians' and this resort to the plural form is scant acknowledgement of the role they played in soliciting, pursuing and preparing the essays. I am grateful to Carla Taines for her speedy and skilful editing of them.

The invitations went out in early Autumn as hard-pressed academics returned to the lecture theatres, and pushed their own writing to fugitive moments between classes, meetings and other commitments. I am particularly indebted to those who found time to take on this additional task, some at very short notice. Several freelance historians were already beholden to deadlines and I thank them for expressing regret that they were not able to contribute. Those represented in this collection agreed that the royalties from this volume would go to *Australian Historical Studies*.

Other colleagues and friends offered their own thoughts on the issues this collection canvasses, and I thank Fay Anderson, Jamie Belich, Frank Bongiorno, Sheila Fitzpatrick and Pat Grimshaw for those conversations. Graeme Powell of the National Library, who for so long has served historical scholarship, answered a number of queries by immediate return of email. He is an exemplar of the values our book affirms.

CONTRIBUTORS

Alan Atkinson writes mainly in the area of colonial Australian history. The first volume of his projected three-volume work, *The Europeans in Australia*, was published in 1997 by Oxford University Press and the second in 2004. He is a Professorial Research Fellow at the University of New England, Armidale.

David Christian taught Russian and World History at Macquarie University in Sydney from 1975 to 2000, when he moved to San Diego State University in California. He has published several books, including a co-authored history of food and drink in Russia, a study of the vodka trade in Russian history, a textbook history of modern Russia, a synoptic history of Russia, Central Asia and Mongolia up to the thirteenth century, and, most recently, a world history that begins with the origins of the Universe and ends in the distant future.

Joy Damousi is Professor in the Department of History at the University of Melbourne. Her recent areas of publication include memory and the history of emotions, themes which she explored in her last two publications, *The Labour of Loss: Mourning, Memory and Wartime Bereavement in Australia* (Cambridge, 1999) and *Living With the Aftermath: Trauma, Nostalgia* *and Grief in Post-war Australia* (Cambridge, 2001), and in the collection of essays edited with Robert Reynolds entitled, *History on the Couch: Essays in History and Psychoanalysis* (MUP, 2003). She is currently writing 'Freud in the Antipodes', a history of psychoanalysis in Australia.

Graeme Davison teaches history at Monash University, where he is a Sir John Monash Distinguished Professor. His books include *The Unforgiving Minute: How Australia Learned to Tell the Time, The Use and Abuse of Australian History, Car Wars: How Cars Won our Hearts and Conquered Our Cities* and, as co-editor, *The Oxford Companion to Australian History*. His prize-winning *The Rise and Fall of Marvellous Melbourne* is to be republished by Melbourne University Publishing in a revised edition in 2004. He has been active for more than twenty years as a writer and advisor on heritage, museums and archives. His current research includes a history of suburban Australia and, as co-editor, a history of Sydney's Power House Museum.

Greg Dening was educated in philosophy, theology, history and anthropology in Jesuit seminaries and at the Universities of Melbourne and Harvard. He has written some dozen books on the cross-cultural history of the Pacific. They include *Islands and Beaches* (1981); *Mr Bligh's Bad Language* (1992); *The Death of William Gooch* (1996); *Performances* (1996); and *Readings/ Writings* (1998). Since his retirement from the Max Crawford Chair of History at the University of Melbourne in 1991, he has been an Adjunct Professor at the Centre for Cross-Cultural Research at the Australian National University. He 'adjuncts' by conducting postgraduate workshops on the creative imagination in the presentation of scholarly knowledge.

John Hirst was born and educated in Adelaide. Since 1968 he has taught history at LaTrobe University. He has written a number of books, among them: *Adelaide and the Country, Convict Society and its Enemies, The Strange Birth of Colonial*

Democracy and *The Sentimental Nation*. He is chair of the Commonwealth government's Civics Education Group and deputy chair of the National Museum Council.

Rhys Isaac is an emeritus professor at LaTrobe University, Melbourne, Australia; and Distinguished Visiting Professor in the History Department of the College of William & Mary, Williamsburg, Virginia. He was born in South Africa in 1937, went to Oxford as a Rhodes Scholar in 1959, and migrated to Australia in 1963. His academic historical specialism is the American Revolution in Virginia. In 1983 his book, *The Transformation of Virginia, 1740–1790* (Chapel Hill, 1982) won the Pulitzer Prize in History. The work employed an anthropological methodology that is associated with the so-called 'Melbourne Group' that includes Greg Dening and Inga Clendinnen. Just published with OUP New York is a book entitled *Landon Carter's Uneasy Kingdom*, that is developed out of the wealth of narrative and cosmological revelation in one of early America's most remarkable long-kept diaries.

Beverley Kingston is a compulsive writer, a constant reader and a frustrated publisher. To support these habits she taught Australian history for thirty years at the University of New South Wales and is now an honorary fellow there. She has written on the history of women's work, on shopping, and a text on the late nineteenth century in Australia which is where she feels she belongs.

Marilyn Lake currently holds a Professorial Research Fellowship at LaTrobe University. Between 2001 and 2002, she held the Chair in Australian Studies at Harvard University and has been appointed to Visiting Fellowships at Stockholm University, the University of Western Australia and the Australian National University. She has published ten books—on subjects ranging from land settlement to feminism; the most recent is a biography of Aboriginal rights activist Faith Bandler, which won the 2002 HREOC prize for non-fiction. Professor Lake writes for newspapers as well as academic journals, and her work has been included in a large number of international anthologies.

Iain McCalman, former director of the Humanities Research Centre at the Australian National University (1995–2003), is currently President of the Australian Academy of the Humanities. He is a Federation Fellow jointly at the Humanities Research Centre and the Centre for Cross-Cultural Research, exploring the life and work of Philippe de Loutherbourg, an eighteenth-century European artist, scientist, engineer and set-designer.

Fiona Paisley is Deputy Director of the Centre for Public Culture and Ideas and Lecturer in Australian History at Griffith University. She is the author of *Loving Protection? Australian Feminism and Aboriginal Women's Rights, 1919–1939* (MUP) and most recently of 'Childhood and race: Growing up in the Empire' in Philippa Levine (ed.), *Gender and Empire* (Oxford University Press, 2004). Her current project concerns gender, race, and cultural internationalism in the Pan-Pacific, 1928–58.

Penny Russell teaches Australian history at the University of Sydney. She is the author of *A Wish of Distinction* (1994) and *This Errant Lady* (2002). Her research interests include governors' wives, identity, status and manners in colonial Australia; and a biographical study of Jane, Lady Franklin. She is passionate about good historical writing.

Glenda Sluga is Associate Professor at the Australian Centre at the University of Melbourne. She has just completed a study of 'Nationality, subjectivity and international history'. She is currently working on an intellectual history of the UN, and an analysis of the nation idea in the work of Germaine de Staël.

STUART MACINTYRE

INTRODUCTION

What are the obligations of the historian? Some would say that the historian is charged with providing knowledge of the past, a knowledge that contributes to an understanding of present circumstances and future possibilities. From this idea of history as a social science comes an expectation of objectivity. The historian is obliged to consider all of the available evidence, subject it to rigorous examination and report the findings dispassionately.

Others take a more emotional view of the past, especially when that past marks out a lineage of achievements and sacrifices that defines identities and commands loyalties. Such is especially the case with national history since it is from formative events in the past that the nation erects its monuments, conducts its ceremonies and draws its ideals. From this idea of history as heritage comes an expectation of custodial responsibility. The historian is obliged to honour the past, to preserve it and keep it alive in the popular memory, to maintain the legacy.

These expectations set up divergent obligations. The one reworks the past to serve the interests of the present, the other attaches the present to a binding past. Historians feel the force of both expectations and respond to both: they have a commitment to investigation of the past, and with that a corresponding duty to conduct their research honestly, while they also are drawn to the past with a deep emotional engagement. The tensions between the two expectations are most likely to create discord in times of rapid change, uncertainty and disagreement, when history offers little guidance to the future and the past no longer binds us—the time in which Thomas Carlyle wrote and our own.

Yet both expectations are surely formulated too starkly. The historian is not simply a researcher who seeks knowledge of the past—for history is concerned with human experience. It is part of the conversation we have with ourselves, an activity that deepens and extends our understanding of the human condition. Nor does history simply beat the bounds of our own identities—it takes us beyond our particular time and place to other worlds and in doing so it enlarges our sympathies and imagination with a fuller appreciation of our common humanity. With these expectations of history as a moral as well as an intellectual discipline and a challenge to our own preferences and assumptions come further obligations of sympathy and humility.

These are some of the ethical obligations of the historian with which this book is concerned. They are qualities that historians seek to practise and by which they evaluate the work of other historians, qualities of good scholarship and good conscience. The moral obligations of the historian bridge the expectations of scrupulous research and respect for the past, yet they too are called into question when the relationship between past and present breaks down in acrimony.

Thomas Carlyle wrote *Past and Present* (1843) as an essay on the condition of England. The pioneer of the industrial revolution, England was full of wealth yet suffered from destitution and discord. From the turmoil of his own times Carlyle cast back to a medieval church community of wise government and honest industry. With the passing of that simple and virtuous way of life, he claimed, went also the faith that sustained it and the ability to understand it. An age dominated by selfishness and egoism saw the heroic figures of the past as fanatics, hypocrites and 'vulturous irrational tyrants'.

'All was insane discord in the Past, brute Force bore rule everywhere. Stupidity, savage Unreason, fitter for bedlam than for a human World!' This was the black armband history that Carlyle accused of defacing the past, and he blamed it on the Enlightenment rationalists. Carlyle practised a different form of history from that of the Dryasdusts, with their arid scholarship and sceptical dogmatism. He sought a higher truth that would teach the great truths of duty and reverence.

It is striking that three of the contributors to this book should draw on Carlyle to affirm the purposes of history. Carlyle appears here as a commentator on the way that historical novels transform the abstractions of historical scholarship into living humanity; as a historian who applied the same skills of imaginative reconstruction to his own writing; and as a critic of progressive orthodoxies who celebrated selfless idealism.

It is also instructive that three present-day historians should make such different uses of this singularly prophetic historian. One of the accusations levelled against the Australian historical profession is that it colludes to deface the past. Building out of the campaign against political correctness, there is the charge that the universities are dominated by radicals who are out of touch with popular values. Arising from the History Wars we have Keith Windschuttle's allegation that an 'orthodox school' of historians has propagated a false and malicious view of the country's past.

The History Wars give an impression of slipshod practice, fabrication of evidence, of dogma replacing fidelity to the factual evidence, collusion in malpractice and misuse of academic procedures to suppress dissent. Attempts to respond to such accusations can take up the questions of accuracy. They can answer the charges of misinterpretation and contest the allegations of bad faith, but many historians are loath to join the History Wars. They feel uncomfortable with the martial metaphor, and its adversarial implications of two opposing forces in combat with each other to control the past. To form ranks and reply to the attack on the history profession is to give a false impression of uniformity.

An alternative response is to go beyond the particular points of contention in the History Wars and extend the narrow terms in which they are formulated. The chief issue debated in the Australian media's coverage of the History Wars—and the History Wars are conducted as a media campaign—involved different calculations of the death toll inflicted by frontier violence. Such a grisly dispute could hardly assist a reckoning with the past. The accusations against the historical profession —for the campaign was intended to discredit historians' troubling account of a settler society's painful relationship with its Indigenous peoples—were that it had tampered with the national story and thereby defaced the past. Such a misunderstanding of history as a monument that cannot be disturbed is indeed a defacement.

The public dispute over Australian history has been conducted for the most part in terms of truth and falsehood. While the motives and integrity of participants are part of that debate, there is surprisingly little attention to the ethical dimensions of historical scholarship. If it is a fundamental duty of the historian to tell the truth, then that scarcely exhausts the obligations that arise when we work with the past. The choice of subject, the engagement with the sources, respect for the evidence, fair dealing with the work of others, attention to context, humility in the exercise of judgement and recognition of what cannot be known—these are just some of the responsibilities a researcher incurs. The mediation between past and present is a profoundly moral activity. Of all the faculties of the historian, a good conscience is indispensable. Technical virtuosity will disguise many flaws, but not bad faith.

An appreciation of these responsibilities is part of the training of the historian. The initial challenge, when we teach, is to explain that history is something more than a fixed body of knowledge, that it is a process of inquiry. We introduce the student to the forms of historical evidence and the procedures that are used to test them. We nurture the skills of historical judgement and interpretation. We encourage students to see how alternative accounts of the past are produced and how they can be assessed. We foster the capacity for independent judgement, originality and imagination that are the hallmarks of good historical scholarship.

Historians profess these qualities in their teaching and research, and they esteem them in the work of their colleagues. The ethical responsibilities of the profession are upheld through its collegial procedures of judgment; they are applied when historians mark an undergraduate essay, examine a thesis, evaluate an application for research funding, assess a manuscript or review a publication. These forms of accountability, however, are mostly bound by rules of confidentiality. They are in-house forms of quality control designed to maintain academic standards and the principles that guide them are seldom exposed to public scrutiny.

As Carlyle insisted and the History Wars attest, the work of historians has more than academic significance. History serves a basic need to know about the past and to understand a range of human experience. It binds nations and shapes the identity of groups within them. It is a form of remembrance and a source of contention. As trained experts, historians make a valuable contribution to these uses of history, but they cannot assume that they stand outside the powerful emotions that attach to the public uses of the past. Nor can they expect a general familiarity with their procedures.

Accordingly we invited a number of historians to take up the ethical issues that arise from their work. The invitation suggested that they might refer to the History Wars but should not be confined to them. From their own experience and from a variety of viewpoints, we asked them to reflect on the obligations of the historian. Among the questions proposed were these:

1. How do historians choose their histories? Are they attracted to congenial subjects? What sort of emotional investment do they make in the subjects they choose to study, and how do they control their sympathies?
2. What balance do historians strike between history as objective knowledge and history as a form of empathetic understanding?
3. On what basis can historians claim such understanding? What are the responsibilities that arise when they enter into the past, when they make the imaginative leap into worlds other than their own? How do they deal with those versions of the past that are powerful markers of present identities?
4. How are historians constrained in their investigations? What sort of obligations are they under to bodies that sponsor their work, or those that control access to information? The practitioners who undertake commissioned history as a professional activity have developed codes of ethics, while research agencies and universities impose ethical requirements on academics: do these help or hinder the historian?
5. How do historians deal with unpalatable discoveries? Do the conventions of quotation and citation provide adequate warrant for the integrity of their writings?

6. Does peer judgement maintain the standards of the profession? How free are historians free to form their own judgements, how far are they bound by orthodoxy?

The invitation was issued to a score or so historians. Those who declined, pleading other commitments, included leading freelance historians. The thirteen whose essays are presented in this volume have pursued their careers within the university. The majority are currently based in the metropolitan centres of Melbourne and Sydney, though some began their careers elsewhere and draw on that experience. They range from distinguished international scholars who have retired from university chairs to mid-career academics. Most work primarily on Australian history but others specialise in different fields.

The essays vary in viewpoint and treatment. Some of the contributors take up particular issues that arise in the practice of history, explore their implications and suggest how the responsibilities of the historian are best discharged. They defend the integrity of the discipline by reasoned argument. Some are more autobiographical, reflecting on their own intellectual journey and the lessons they have learned. They offer lessons in historical understanding. Some make direct reference to the History Wars and some prefer to keep their distance.

Alan Atkinson notes that one of the criticisms made against Keith Windschuttle's treatment of Aboriginal deaths in *The Fabrication of Aboriginal History* was an absence of sympathy. When I put it to Keith Windschuttle last year that his account of what had happened in colonial Tasmania lacked compassion, he replied that the duty of the historian was to be dispassionate. Atkinson observes that this disagreement seemed to be marginal to the dispute that Windschuttle's book created, and insists that compassion is in fact good history's main motive.

He sees history as a moral discipline that enlarges our understanding of humanity and extends our human sympathy.

Atkinson traces this humanitarian sensibility to the Enlightenment, linked to the expansion of Europe, the growth of
the market and the formation of civil society. He finds it in the
writings of conservatives such as Edmund Burke and the scepticism of Edward Gibbon, whose condemnation of 'the cool
unfeeling historian' seems to anticipate Carlyle's censure of
the Dryasdusts. That dispassionate school of history turned the
study of the past into a branch of the social sciences, emphasis-
ing an objectivity that separated the investigator from the subject, and Atkinson welcomes the recent revival of emotional
history. He warns of its difficulties, insists that feeling has to be
combined with careful thought—qualities that he finds in a
number of works on Australian history and exemplifies in his
own work on *The Europeans in Australia*.

Joy Damousi is just one of the other contributors who take
up the involvement of emotions in history. As she puts it, the
scientific school of history sought to understand the past as a
form of objective knowledge and to provide a rational explanation of human behaviour. Personal feeling was discounted as
subjective and irrational, personal memory as idiosyncratic
and unreliable. Those historians suppressed emotions in order
to get at the truth, but now the repressed resurfaces. Rather
than treating history and memory as antonyms, Damousi argues
that it is necessary to respect the personal truths of memory
and incorporate them into historical interpretation. Where
these personal memories arise out of traumatic events, the
process becomes a form of therapeutic history.

Emotions provide a point of entry into history, a way of
engaging with and responding to the past. Greg Dening recalls
the impact of his encounter with two foundational documents
in the National Library, the two Australian contributions to the
Memory of the World Register. As a leading Pacific historian
he was familiar with the published journal of James Cook's first
great voyage of 1768–71, which took the English navigator

first to Tahiti to observe the transit of Venus and then to New Zealand and the eastern coast of Australia. But as he turned the pages of the original that Cook wrote fresh from experience, his pen trembling with emotion, Dening was transported into the cabin on the *Endeavour*. As he examined the drawings that Eddie Mabo made of his ancestral islands, documents that would jolt Australian legal history into a new awareness, Dening made the imaginative leap into a Deep Time that is known through story, dance, ritual and life experience.

How do we acquire such historical imagination? It seems to come from empathy and intuition in a creative encounter with the remains of the past that takes the historian into another world. Some contributors make reference to the formative influence of historical novels of Walter Scott and Robert Louis Stevenson, though Iain McCalman insists on the need to distinguish fiction from fact. Penny Russell observes that the discipline of history lies between those branches of knowledge such as science and medicine that deal with the real and those that such as literature, art and music that deal with the creative imagination. History works on the emotions. The writing of history involves working and reworking the raw material of reality into a finished form that reveals something more. But for historians, Russell reminds us, the truth will always get in the way of a good story—and make the story better.

Historians find their raw material in the archives. They have a commitment to immerse themselves in the documentary record. Several of the contributors attest to the labour this imposes, with the relevant material heaped up in repositories that are widely scattered and often require lengthy visits. Yet there is no other way. Greg Dening attests to the compulsion to see everything there is to be seen, and likens it to the insistence of anthropologists on ethnographic fieldwork: the historian's feeling for the past is determined by the hours, days, months and years spent sitting in the archives. It is small wonder that Iain McCalman should be so disconcerted by the suggestion of a reviewer that he invented the dialogue in his recent book on an eighteenth-century adventurer, Count Cagliostro, since every quotation had been assembled from a lengthy search of European manuscript collections.

Beverley Kingston attests to the painstaking craft of archival research. She describes how she appraises the material for provenance and context before selecting passages for summary and copying out quotations, how she organises her notes and verifies them, and how she establishes a hierarchy of sources. Kingston conducts her own research and avoids such short-cuts as photocopying, since that merely delays the necessary engagement with the material. She believes that these standards are under pressure in universities that require research to cover its costs, encourage the delegation of data collection to assistants and encourage premature publication of slipshod work.

I'm not sure that all of her fears are warranted. Funding agencies do not restrict support to research that will yield a return on the outlay, and if they did disciplines such as astronomy would be hit harder than history. Some research projects benefit from collaboration, and research assistants can make a valuable contribution. The pressure to publish is tempered by the processes of evaluation. Yet Kingston is surely right in her insistence that there is no substitute for the sustained and systematic attention to the sources. Rhys Isaac echoes her with his own observation that history is better than fable only if it is founded on the complex documentary record of the past.

Historians declare their fidelity to the record of the past in references, and these too are discussed by several of the contributors. The references tell the reader what sources have been used; they specify the precise location of a quotation or the particular documents that have been used in the reconstruction of an incident. They are appended to the text, traditionally in footnotes at the bottom of the page and more commonly now in endnotes at the back of the book, though the older term is used generically. Footnotes tie the interpretation to the evidence, and identify the evidence exactly so it can be checked and confirmed. As such, they are an essential safeguard of scholarly integrity, the basis of the reader's trust that the historian is not simply making it up.

But footnotes can also give a false impression of certainty; as Penny Russell observes, they can intimidate the reader with a vaunting display of erudition. She prefers footnotes that take the reader back to the evidence with a humility that allows the possibility of other interpretations, a usage that Graeme Davison endorses. He draws on the insight of Anthony Grafton in his recent examination of the footnote, that it turns monologue into dialogue and opens up a conversation between the writer and the reader, the historian and the evidence.

This is one reason, I suspect, why historians retain a preference for footnotes over the method of giving references in the text by the author-date system that is now standard in the sciences and social sciences. Footnotes allow the historian to acknowledge obligations to the work of others, or to indicate points of disagreement with that work. They widen the conversation to take in the relevant historical literature and in doing so they augment trust that the historian is familiar with the subject and bound by the conventions of the discipline. Here too the footnotes qualify the impression of omniscience with a recognition that alternative interpretations exist and others are possible.

From this interplay between the creative imagination and the conventions of historical scholarship the contributors reflect on how their sympathies enter into their history and how they control them. These encounters reveal a variety of challenges to the historian's conscience.

Fiona Paisley writes of her discoveries in the archives of shocking material on the treatment of Aboriginal Aboriginals. Some of it she finds too painful to publish, while she has used other sensitive material with caution and misgiving. How was she drawn to such a difficult subject? She thinks back to her teenage days in Nowra, when she was unaware of the Aboriginal presence, and reflects on the way that non-Indigenous people can share space with Indigenous people and not see them, how they can share histories and understand them differently. She thinks her own desire to make good this separation was shaped by her family background. An immigrant herself, she believes her research interests speak of a desire to find an ethical way to be an Anglo-Celtic Australian settler colonial.

Glenda Sluga reflects similarly on the way her family history influenced first her study of the Bonegilla migrant reception centre and then her consideration of the troubled history of Trieste, where her parents lived before coming to Australia. Trieste is a border region, its history tangled up in ethnic conflict and the Cold War, and those sensitivities persist in the migrant communities of Australia as well as the reception of her work. In her case it was the refusal to take sides that caused offence. She reminds us of the international and transnational dimensions of the History Wars, and the ethical responsibilities they present.

Marilyn Lake considers the further challenge of sympathy for unsympathetic subjects. She began her career, she says, by taking sides and came to see that the greater challenge was to understand. First in her history of Australian feminism she had to deal with an earlier generation of women activists whose views on many subjects were uncongenial; now in her work on those who sought to make Australia, along with other settler societies, into a white man's country, she confronts the elevation of race into a national ideal. History, she argues, cannot be written as a story of heroes and villains; it has to create a more complex understanding that enables us to see why these aspirations flourished.

If Lake was surprised to find her sympathies identified with those of her subjects, John Hirst feels that his history writing has changed his views—or perhaps his sympathies have changed his history. He learned his history from left-wing teachers and began his career as a Labor supporter, only to find as he studied political history that he was a pragmatist. When he turned to convict history he was influenced by some revisionist work on American slavery, but also by his experience as the father of a rebellious teenage son and his growing concern for the maintenance of authority. He was criticised for failing to denounce the cruel punishment of convicts, but he was reluctant to judge the past by the standards of the present. Here is a remarkably accomplished historian declaring the subjectivity of his work, as well as its potency.

The contributors are by no means agreed on the significance of their work. Beverley Kingston makes a plea for modesty. Historians possess no particular authority, she writes, and despite their appeals to professional status 'no training is really required to research or write history'. Bad history, she adds, does not have the same consequences as a faulty bridge or a wrongly diagnosed illness, where the professional expertise of the engineer or medical graduate is vital. At worst it will only deceive and affront.

Greg Dening puts it differently. He found his vocation as a young historian when he discovered he wanted to write of the Pacific peoples on the other side of the beach, the islanders who seemed to have little wealth or power, and left few records of their own. He wanted to hear their voices and celebrate their creativity, and he applied himself to acquiring the forms of knowledge that would enable him to do so. Dening recalls the excitement of that quest, and the feeling that 'the past belonged to us because we had the skills to discover it'—then his realisation that the past belongs to those on whom it impinges.

Rhys Isaac follows the implications of that insight. As a student in South Africa during the 1950s, he too aspired to a more inclusive history than that of empire and settlement. With Greg Dening and Inga Clendinnen he enlarged the history of colonisation into a two-sided history, of the colonised as well as the colonisers. He sees this urge to enlarge history, to cross the boundaries of the white man's historiography and write about the other side of the frontier, as having both ethical and intellectual impulses. It was shaped by the democratising moral reassessments that accompanied decolonisation and it was made possible by new methods of reconstructing other ways of living and acting.

Isaac illustrates how these moral and intellectual obligations came together in a museum in the town of Williamsburg in the State of the Virginia. As a leading historian of colonial Virginia, he has been closely involved in guiding the museum while it negotiated the sensitivities of the past, especially the dispossession of Native Americans and the institution of slavery. The disagreements were resolved not by flinching from the past, but by involving those who felt strongly about it, by consulting, negotiating and joining the most troublesome episodes to a larger, more inclusive narrative.

From this case study it is apparent that the past impinges on many people and no single group has exclusive possession of it. It is also apparent that the historian plays a vital role in assisting occupancy. Isaac tells us that his research was directed by 'an urge to make those other histories' and it was his expertise in them that allowed him to guide the work of the museum. What happens when the claimants to the past are unwilling to share it, when the authority of the historian allows no such resolution?

This is the impasse that Graeme Davison describes in his account of the recent controversy in the National Museum. As he recounts, the museum was subjected to criticism from those who thought it insufficiently affirmative of the national achievement. They criticised its exhibitions, challenged its guidelines, pressured its director, secured an external review and in other ways interfered with its operation as a public institution. Davison distinguishes between three models of the museum, the first imposed by the government as an authorised presentation of the national past, the second the product of institutional consensus, and the third his preferred model of civic pluralism where different interpretations open up discussion of the past.

He reminds us of the expectations that arise when historians work in such public settings. Their own standards of judgement, the tests they apply to their own writings and the writings of colleagues, can no longer be assumed. Public institutions that serve the wider community have other responsibilities, so that community values have to be reconciled with expert opinion. In Davison's first model the historian is expected to follow the bidding of the government, in his second to work within some broadly negotiated framework.

Historians helped devise the original charter of the National Museum, and the guidelines that Davison himself drafted suggested it would celebrate and challenge. Davison also reviewed the exhibit labels after they were criticised, and subjected to them to tests of accuracy and fairness. He did not expect to agree with them and asked simply that they were consistent with reputable scholarship. This pluralism was unacceptable to the champions of the first model.

David Christian enlarges on the way that history serves the nation. While many of our interests and concerns cross national boundaries, the nation retains a tenacious hold on loyalties. One way it does so is with history. Historians helped form and bind nations through the powerful stories they told and governments, he says, ensure that they are passed down to future citizens in their school lessons. It is salutary to be reminded that Manning Clark was a patriotic historian, though some readers will wish that this nation's schools were more attentive to the past.

Historians feel other pressures, other temptations. Some contributors note how the book industry encourages simplification of scholarship, popularisation of content and a degree of certainty that the historian is reluctant to claim. Marilyn

Lake explains that her publisher insisted on the definite article in the subtitle of her book, *Getting Equal*: not *A history of Australian feminism*, as she wanted, but *The history*. Beverley Kingston reminds us that some historians do not have to be tempted to press their claims for attention.

Iain McCalman's account of writing popular history is the fullest of these cautionary tales. He set out to write a book for the trade, not an academic monograph aimed at the academy but a much different one for the general reading market. Some of his expectations were confounded. His editor wasn't worried by the footnotes, allowed the title *The Seven Ordeals of Count Cagliostro* and was prepared to accept there could be seven viewpoints on the Count, but did not want McCalman to affront his readers with vulgarities. Most alarming was the way the editor referred to the book as 'your novel' and suggested plot enhancements that had no historical warrant.

This, then, was the eighth ordeal of Iain McCalman and it strengthened his conviction that historians have an absolute obligation to historical truth. He does not suggest that he has written *the* truth about Cagliostro but he does insist that his book is not fiction, that it is bound by the sources and follows the proper procedures of interpretation. It is on such respect for the past that the historical enterprise rests, and the historian's conscience is satisfied.

CHAPTER 1

ALAN ATKINSON

DO GOOD HISTORIANS HAVE FEELINGS?

In reading our way through Australia's History Wars we often see the work of revisionists condemned as chilling or cruel. But the condemnation rarely amounts to an argument. It is usually meant as a kind of supplement to the writer's main points. However valid it might be as a moral judgement, from a scholarly point of view it is not clear what weight it is meant to carry. Robert Manne, writing in the *Sydney Morning Herald* about Keith Windschuttle's *The Fabrication of Aboriginal History*, volume one, remarks on its 'pitilessness' but then he quickly passes, in the same sentence, to a detailed account of the book's 'internal self-contradictions'. In *Australian Historical Studies* Stuart Macintyre sets the same work within the broad sweep of history-writing since the eighteenth century and then similarly goes on, in his final sentences (about the counting of deaths), to suggest that while historians might disagree on such points, 'at the very least we expect to find sympathy and compassion for the victims. I do not see it', he observes, 'in this book'.[1]

Thanks to Frank Bongiorno for his comments on this essay.

So what? Does the presence or absence of sympathy and compassion affect the quality of a piece of historical scholarship? Or are such statements really superfluous to the central task? I argue here on one side only. Far from being superfluous, compassion (I leave sympathy aside) is good history's main motive.

All scholarship can be weighed and understood as a social activity. It is anchored in shared habits of thought, in custom and communication. It not only takes place among human beings. It is also, in every way, an expression of community. But more than that again, it is mainly about human beings. It is a means of exploring, and also extending, the dimensions of humanity. History is one of those modern disciplines whose basic principles were set out during the European Enlightenment, the first age of humanitarianism. It qualifies as one of the humanities because it examines human experience and because it is a means of enlarging humane imagination. In a broad sense, it began as, and it still is, a moral discipline.

I mean 'moral' in an eighteenth-century as well as a nineteenth- and twentieth-century sense, in that collective and social—even ethnographic—sense still obvious in terms like 'morale' and 'moral economy'. This package of meaning was not really possible before the eighteenth century, because only then did collective humanity begin to be interesting and to make moral claims in its own right. In 1985 the American scholar Thomas Haskell published a powerful argument on the causes of eighteenth-century humanitarianism. He wrote of a shift in 'cognitive style', in ways of perceiving the world and of dealing with humanity at a distance from oneself. The result was 'a new moral universe', a more complex and extended sense of moral responsibility. Haskell attributed this change to the way European imagination began to embrace wider patterns of cause and effect, largely as a result of the world-wide distribution of European capital and the stronger sense of agency which went with ubiquitous planning and investment. Men and women began to understand that their own actions might affect the lives of strangers much more than they could have done hitherto. A sense of commercial responsibility, said Haskell, gave rise to a sense of humanitarian responsibility.[2]

Haskell was mainly concerned to explain the rise of the anti-slavery movement. In doing so he explored the mystery of the suffering stranger—why do we, and why did humanitarians in the eighteenth century, feel moved to take deliberate action with the idea of helping men, women and children we and they never met?[3] But he left out large aspects of the question. Enlightenment thought not only increased the *geographical* reach of humane imagination. It did the same across stretches of time, with historical competence. It not only widened the European sense of *active* moral responsibility. It also deepened feelings of moral involvement with strangers who could not be helped at all because, at least in many cases, they were long dead. Some, in fact, had never lived at all. They were fictional. The rise of the novel, which was closely tied to the rise of historical narrative, had a profound effect on sensibility of this kind.

'Responsibility' is still the right word. Historians thus began, if very slowly, to take on the multifaceted labours sketched out above, so as to be accountable in various directions at once. It is possible to suggest invidious distinctions between moral responsibility tied to deliberate action, as with anti-slavery, and moral responsibility which is expressed in thought, speech and writing, about events long past and events which never really happened. The latter is surely the moral responsibility of the mere 'bleeding heart'. But in fact the two belong together. Humanitarianism relates to both humans and animals. In just the same way it involves both action and thought. All are parts of a single pattern of sensibility.

Edmund Burke was an Enlightenment thinker. In his own way, he was also an advocate of humanitarianism, as an aspect of collective humanity and civilised imagination. Burke was speaking of all forms of scholarship when he said in 1790 that nothing 'can give true weight and sanction to any learned opinion [but] . . . the common nature and common relations of men'.[4] In other words, historians are accountable, by Enlightenment criteria, to those who read or otherwise consume their work, as with any tradesman or manufacturer who places products in the market. But they also work within a wider and more diffuse body of moral opinion. Like medical practitioners, they are accountable to their subject matter, because that subject matter is human. And beyond that Burke's reference to 'the common nature and common relations of men' brings in the larger question of community.

Burke made a great deal of the virtues of civilised community, or, as he called it, civil society. He thought of intellectual achievement as something completely shaped and determined by collective existence. After the statement already quoted he went on to explain that 'without civil society man could not by any possibility arrive at the perfection of which his nature is capable [and he meant perfection of all kinds], nor even make a remote and faint approach to it'.[5] This sounds like platitude. But workers in the humanities, in deciding why and how they do their job, are really obliged to think about the mechanics of the cause–effect relationship outlined by Burke. What is the exact connection between civil society and good argument about the past?

Common humanity, as it was defined by the best Enlightenment writers, partly involved shared feeling. The brilliant impact of Edward Gibbon's *Decline and Fall of the Roman Empire*, another Enlightenment work, was partly owing to the fact that the author wrote with an unprecedented vividness. His style might seem latinate and courtly to later generations, but its success was a result of the way in which he entered into the common emotional experience of the people he wrote about. Gibbon's own emotions were central too. Humanitarianism of the kind he subscribed to involved a nakedness of feeling which exposed the human quality of the writer himself. 'The bloody actor', said Gibbon (and he meant anyone who acts a violent part on the stage of history), 'is less detestable than the cool unfeeling historian'.[6] The intellectual power of Gibbon's work depended on its emotional energy. *Decline and Fall of the Roman Empire* is a work of compassion, in the original sense of the word—of shared feeling, something larger than sympathy or pity. 'Empathy' might be a better word, except that it too means less now than it once did. A combination of intellectual and emotional force makes Gibbon's book a subtle and penetrating account of humanity. The result, in Enlightenment terms, is fundamentally moral.

It is easy to see now that Enlightenment writers, such as Gibbon, did not make enough allowance for the diversity of emotional and cultural experience among peoples. They assumed that human feeling always took the same form, whatever the time and place. They took too little account of the varying impact of cultural circumstances. During the nineteenth century the tendency was just the opposite. It was understood then, in reaction to Enlightenment doctrine, that feeling varied enormously—that intense feeling, for instance, was proof of high civilisation. It followed that the poor and ill-educated had duller feelings than the rich and refined. Other types of humanity were also supposed to feel less than Europeans did. Charles Dickens gives a picture of this attitude in *David Copperfield*, when he describes the villain of the story, the gentleman Steerforth, talking about the poor—'that sort of people'. 'Why, there's a pretty wide separation between them and us', says Steerforth, '. . . they are not to be expected to be as sensitive as we are. Their delicacy is not to be shocked, or hurt very easily . . . they have not very fine natures; and they may be thankful that, like their coarse rough skins, they are not easily wounded'.[7] As for feeling and race, Keith Windschuttle offers a fairly precise reflection of nineteenth-century ideas when he himself states that the Tasmanian Aborigines necessarily lacked 'humanity and compassion'. These were 'concepts', says Windschuttle, which 'they would have regarded with complete incomprehension . . . It was the European

Enlightenment that founded the idea of the unity of humanity and the Christian religion that originated the notion of sharing the suffering of others.'[8] Such feelings were therefore beyond the Tasmanians.

Obviously, the search for difference can be too eager and too absolute. It ought to be clear from both these examples (Dickens meant it to be clear) that too much cultural relativism weakens common humanity, which is not only a moral but also (the main point of this essay) an intellectual failing. Historians who deny or who minimise feeling in their subjects, and/or their own participation in that feeling, write under a self-imposed disability. Gibbon was right to condemn, as a destroyer of life, including intellectual life, the 'cool unfeeling historian'. At the same time, historical writing has moved forward and Gibbon's dictum has been qualified by other insights, especially since about the 1970s. In 1985 Peter and Carol Stearns published in the *American Historical Review* an account of the progress of what they called 'Emotionology', the new study of the history of feeling.

> [S]ocieties [they said] have emotional standards. Anthropologists have long known and studied this phenomenon. Historians are increasingly aware of it, as we realize that the emotional standards of societies change in time rather than merely differ, constantly, across space. Changes in emotional standards can in turn reveal much about other aspects of social change and may even contribute to such change.[9]

'Standards' might seems a curious term here. It betrays a belief in absolute measures of feeling, characteristic of what was then the new sub-discipline of psycho-history—at least insofar as clinical ideas about emotional health were applied to past societies. The former psychiatrist Lloyd de Mause, for instance, had used his book, *The History of Childhood* (1974), to argue that the feelings of parents for their children were typically much more impoverished in the past than they were in the present. This idea of variety has a lasting importance. Also de Mause's suggestion of a progressive refinement in sensibility was an improvement on the dichotomous ideas—us and them —of previous days. But more recently again, the best scholarship has moved beyond the one-dimensional implications of work like his.

To repeat—writing history, or presenting it in any form, is a social activity. It depends on an assumption of shared humanity. That assumption involves feeling, and not just as an ornament and selling point. It follows that historians who fail to register the importance of feeling, whether explicitly or not, cut themselves off from the roots of their discipline.

Gibbon might rail against the 'unfeeling historian' but it took two hundred years for scholars to begin to come to terms with what a 'feeling historian' might be like. During most of the nineteenth and twentieth centuries there seemed to be an urgent need to think of history-writing not as a social activity but as a science. Scientific knowledge was then the supreme index of truth and professional respectability. Legitimacy, as so often during that time, depended on the refinement of technique—in the case of historians, on thorough, accurate documentation and on objectivity, a clear line between subject (researchers) and object (their material). Peter and Carol Stearns joked in passing about 'the historian of emotions' and 'the emotional historian', as if the two were utterly distinct. They looked forward, in 1985, to a type of scholarship which took full account of feeling. And yet they still resisted the possibility that their own feelings might be matched and compared with those they wrote about. History was to remain nothing more or less than a body of steadily accumulating, solid information. It was not to be understood in terms of accountability to human subjects and to readership. In principle, once again, there was only one obvious ethical question. Was the writing correctly tied to the evidence? Keith Windschuttle, harking back to the habits of an earlier age, makes the

point perfectly: 'I'm trying to find the truth of the matter . . .
My self is really irrelevant in this'.[10]

As I say, historical scholarship has come a long way since
1985. Few good historians could now write about the study of
past emotion as the Stearnses did then. 'One of the challenges
of research in this field', they said, 'is to sort out the durable
(animal) from the transient (culturally caused)'.[11] For them the
'durable' and universal aspects of emotion must be understood
in biological terms. Common humanity was not to be a factor
in explaining motivation—it was to be manifest only in physical form, the bodily shape of *homo sapiens*. With this understanding historians kept themselves at a distance from their
subject matter, denying the existence of feelings shared. It is
easy, on looking back, to understand their fears. The scientist
resists being dissected. But since that time historians, in
moving forward, have also made their way back to the foun-
dations of the discipline, back past the priorities of technique
to the priorities of humanity. The overwhelming sense of
global humanity which has developed since the 1980s, and
which reflects and revives some of the key concerns of the
Enlightenment, makes a statement like the one just quoted
seem a little ridiculous.

The same period has seen the burgeoning of Aboriginal
history in Australia. The revived interest in feeling, as a historical phenomenon and as something central to the way
history ought to be understood, has been part of the cause,
though mostly an implicit part. Henry Reynolds set the pace
in a number of ways but he has not been completely typical of
writers—or readers—on this subject. The main connecting
theme in Reynolds' work is violent dispossession and resulting
problems of justice. His arguments lead straight into questions
of legality. But questions of feeling, especially suffering, have
otherwise dominated the field. Aboriginal history is emotional

history. Its usual purpose is to make an emotional point, or rather to make an intellectual point sharpened and coloured by emotion. There are other, comparable types of subject matter, such as the trench experience of World War I—Bill Gammage's book, *The Broken Years* (1974), is a wonderful instance—and the prisoner-of-war experience of World War II. Joy Damousi tackles the issue of wartime and post-war grieving in her book, *The Labour of Loss* (1999). Perhaps it has been women's history most of all which, in Australia, has legitimised the history of feeling. Miriam Dixson's *The Real Matilda* (1976) was another powerful early experiment in the history of emotion.

It ought to go without saying that many studies of feeling are superficial and inept—even, with the best intentions, patronising. Feeling can undermine as well as justify careful thought. Writers sometimes assume a degree or quantity of suffering which they cannot wholly prove. Some seem to think that the capacity to feel is all they need. Some only write about the kind of suffering which it seems easy to appreciate—physical pain and the loss of land and family, for instance. Other issues of emotional trauma might be ignored because of a lack of skill in dealing with them, although the damage may be deeper and more permanent. In Australia, success so far is uneven, partly because writers have not always understood the novelty and difficulty of what they are trying to do. A lot can be learnt from writers like Inga Clendinnen—from the extraordinary combination of moral sensibility and self-discipline which appears, for instance, in her book *Reading the Holocaust* (1998). But taken as a whole such essays in the history of feeling add up to a magnificent leap forward for Australian scholarship.

Fiction writers are much more experienced in this area. Maybe for that reason attempts by historians to focus on feeling can read like fiction—and can be condemned in those terms. Certainly many historians, trained at a time when history seemed to be a kind of science, draw a clear line between fiction and their own type of learning. And yet historical novels can uncover large truths about the past just as effectively as history wholly attached to the evidence. Nineteenth-century history was inspired in essential ways by the historical fiction of Sir Walter Scott—*Waverley, Ivanhoe, Rob Roy* and so on—because in his writing Scott proved the palpable humanity of the people he described. Thomas Carlyle described Scott as the discoverer of a new 'continent in Literature'.

> [T]hese Historical Novels [said Carlyle] have taught all men this truth, which looks like a truism, and yet was as good as unknown to writers of history and others, till so taught: that the bygone ages of the world were actually filled by living men, not by protocols, state-papers, controversies and abstractions of men. Not abstractions were they, not diagrams and theorems; but men.

Anyone who has taught undergraduates will know how much labour it still takes sometimes to convert the apparent cardboard thinness of past humanity into flesh and blood. 'It is a little word this;' said Carlyle, 'inclusive of great meaning! History will henceforth have to take thought of it.'[12] We are still struggling to take thought of it.

The History Wars has been described as a game of Left versus Right. It does echo those old battles, but only in superficial ways. There are some real breaks of continuity. After all, it was the Right, not the Left, which used to argue the importance of communion between past and present. Also, a pattern of ideas anchored in the work of men like Gibbon and Burke cannot be called left-wing. No, this is really a debate about compassion (in a broad sense). It overlaps with current affairs and with large contemporary issues of ethical debate. Is compassion necessary in discussing the experience of other human beings? In what circumstances can their emotions be ignored?

What then is the importance of humane feeling within the humanities? This is barely an ideological issue at all. It is a moral one. It goes to the foundation of intellectual life and beyond that, as Burke would say, to the character of civil society.

NOTES

1. Robert Manne, 'Blind to truth, and blind to history', *Sydney Morning Herald*, 16 December 2002; Stuart Macintyre, 'History, politics and the philosophy of history', *Australian Historical Studies*, vol. 30, no. 123 (April), 2004, p. 136.

2. Thomas L. Haskell, 'Capitalism and the origins of the humanitarian sensibility' (in two parts), *American Historical Review*, vol. 90, 1985.

3. See also Michael Ignatieff, *The Needs of Strangers*, Chatto & Windus, London, 1984 .

4. Edmund Burke, *Reflections on the Revolution in France*, Walter Scott Publishing, London, n.d., p. 121.

5. Burke, p. 122.

6. Edward Gibbon, *The History of the Decline and Fall of the Roman Empire*, ed. David Womersley, Allen Lane, London: 1994, vol. 2, p. 147 (originally vol. 3, chapter 30, fn. 82).

7. Charles Dickens, *David Copperfield*, Penguin, Harmondsworth, 1966, p. 352.

8. Keith Windschuttle, *The Fabrication of Aboriginal History*, volume one, *Van Diemen's Land 1803–1847*, Macleay Press, Sydney, 2002, p. 406.

9. Peter N. Stearns and Carol Z. Stearns, 'Emotionology: Clarifying the history of emotions and emotional standards', *American Historical Review*, vol. 90, 1985, p. 814.

10. Windschuttle, quoted in Andrew Stevenson, 'A voice from the frontier', *Spectrum*, p. 8, *Sydney Morning Herald*, 22–23 September 2002.

11. Stearns and Stearns, p. 824.

12. Thomas Carlyle, 'Sir Walter Scott', in his *Critical and Miscellaneous Essays*, vol. 4, Chapman & Hall, London, 1899, pp. 77–8.

CHAPTER 2

JOY DAMOUSI

THE EMOTIONS OF HISTORY

In a lyrical review of *French Children of the Holocaust: A Memorial*, Thomas Laqueur identifies a tension at the very heart of writing history. On the one hand, he observes, the aim of history is to be objective and factual, to construct a narrative that is rational, cool, and aspires towards achieving some truth. On the other, there are the claims of memory, which are subjective, emotional, and contest any universalist notion of a truth.[1] Daniel Abramson summarises these paradigms in another way: 'Memory privileges the private and the emotional, the subjective and the bodily. Against history's officialism, memory recalls hidden pasts, the lived, the local, the ordinary and the every day. Against history's totality, memory is the key to personal and collective identity'.[2] Which is the more ethical way of writing history: with a distance and analytical eye or with a subjective compassion and overt empathy towards one's subject?

In recent times these debates have been played out most dramatically in historical writings on the Holocaust. Saul Friedlander identifies the issue in terms of whether the emotional involvement in the events of the Holocaust precludes writing a 'rational' history. 'The "mythic memory" of the victims', he observes, 'has been set against the "rational under-standing" of others'. While a degree of transference by the historian is unavoidable and at times desirable, he argues 'the historian should be attuned to complexity and not avoid the precise definition of interpretative concepts and categories, especially in the domain so wide open to extraordinary flights of imagination or malicious denials'.[3]

Most historians would try to move beyond these polarities and achieve what Laqueur describes as the 'shimmering tension' between these two claims of history: to combine the two and 'speak both to historical distance and to the immediacy of memory'.[4]

Lying beneath the surface of these debates is also the issue of the role of emotions in historical writing. Writing in 1935, the philosopher R. G. Collingwood reflected on whether emotions can be a part of history. Collingwood argued that history is a story about thought and rational life. 'Many human emotions', he reflects,

> are certainly bound up with the spectacle of . . . life in its vicissi-tudes . . . but this is not history . . . [T]he record of immediate experience with its flow of sensations and feelings, faithfully preserved in a diary or recalled in a memoir, is not history. At its best, it is poetry; at its worst, an obtrusive egotism; but history it can never be.[5]

History began as a form of literature that worked on the emotions and tried to show the fickleness of fate and how humans had reacted to it. It evoked wonder, awe, horror and admiration. It developed as a way of civilising instinct, chan-nelling and controlling emotions. In the turn to the scientific school, historians sought to suppress emotions. But now the repressed resurfaces. Collingwood's view been challenged, although there are many historians who would still agree with him. It is undeniable that historians continue to have an attach-ment to stories of rationality; they invariably consider emotions as either tangential, or irrational and therefore irrelevant to historical inquiry, politics or culture.[6] Emotions are also treated as part of the messiness of human life, that which has to be cut away to get at the substance of history.

The tension between emotions and facts, the subjective and objective, also raises a number of ethical questions surrounding 'truth'. How do we deal with our own emotional investments in our histories if historical endeavours are meant to be the objective pursuit of the 'truth'? How do we write about the emotions of others in historic accounts? In the case of the former, I would argue that examining our own empathies certainly requires a considerable degree of self-reflexivity. But it also demands that we examine the cultural, political and social processes at work as well. In the latter case, the balance between respecting memory as a person's *truth* and subjecting it to the rigors of historical categories and interpretation is surely what is desired. I want to draw on the example of the recent pilgrimages to the Anzac battlefront to explore the perplexing nexus between emotions, memory, history and ethics. The broad point I wish to make is that ethics in history is tied to the political—broadly defined—and that the world of emotions and memory also need to be understood within this rubric. If the new ethics in history require an 'openness to testimony'[7]—of bearing witness to another's trauma or inequality or pain through memory— then the ethical responsibility of the historian is not only to document such responses but also to identify the forces which produced the conditions for these testimonies. It follows that we should resist efforts to normalise memory and should rescue what is forgotten as well as what is remembered.

It has been estimated that between 13 000 and 16 000 Australians undertook the trip to Gallipoli each year between 2000 and 2002. Most of them had no family connections with the battle and were not veterans themselves. Few who attended these pilgrimages had much knowledge of the military campaigns or political history of the World War I. And yet the numbers of pilgrims continue to grow, particularly through testimonies on the internet. As journalist Michelle Griffin notes, 'Gallipoli is not just a myth; it's an idea generated by the internet age'.[8] This campaigning has become a systematic ritual and occasion where the heroism, sacrifice and commitment of soldiers are celebrated. The horror of war is recalled, the prime minister honours the dead, and sacrifices are acknowledged. This is a secularised ritual in an age when our society has very few rituals to define its identity.

But what in fact is being remembered and forgotten of Australia's past? Anzac Day marks the anniversary of the event which, in popular mythology, symbolises Australia's nationhood. This commemoration serves to consolidate what Lyn Spillman refers to as a 'founding moment' of nation.[9] What do these travellers find in the story of Anzac, when they travel to the war graves and battlefield and join in this ritual of collective memory? As Bruce Scates has convincingly argued, the compelling attraction of the pilgrimage is a spiritual one, where the participants are bound by the emotions of the moment and a sense of belonging and community. By inventing a ritual of this sort, which shows respect and honours those who gave their lives, those of a new generation discover what they perceive to be a sense of national identity and cultural meaning.[10]

This collective memory can also be considered from another perspective, through another genre which defines this experience—that of the pilgrim as tourist. In his reminiscences of his experience of pilgrimage from Sydney to Turkey, the journalist Tony Wright records his thoughts and reflections on what those like himself gathered to do on Anzac Day in 2002 on the Gallipoli Peninsula.

> Alone among nations, we had chosen our one consecrated day not to trumpet a victory, but to remember ancestors who had suffered

and died trying . . . In choosing Anzac Day as the most important
national day of the year . . . Australians and New Zealanders were
not celebrating war. They were remembering . . . [those] who did
not give up, even in defeat.[11]

How would a historian observe this occasion differently?
The ethical responsibility of the historian would be to consider *how* and *why* the expression of these sentiments and
emotions construct a particular narrative of Anzac. Such an
analysis would move beyond the journalist's ethic to evoke
and capture the moment, into an interpretation of politics and
history. 'Anzac', it can be argued, becomes a generic and universalist story of celebrating the triumph of the human spirit
against impossible odds; it becomes an inspiring story of the
power of courage, endurance, mateship and heroism. The
Anzac story is about those who 'died trying', who 'did not
give up even in defeat'. The public memory of this event, and
the sense of the past that is derived from Anzac, is, a historian
might suggest, based less on the specificities of historical
understanding than on a generalised experience of pain and
suffering. In rewriting this as a generic tale, it would be beholden on the historian to suggest what is missing in this
commemorative moment: the imperialist and colonial aspirations of the British Empire which evaporate from an effort to
universalise the story; an understanding of the xenophobia
which underpins war; the very reasons why and how war
happens remains unexamined in these commemorations. The
complexity of war, with its multiple battles, and the multitude
of stories and myths that emerge from them, is lost in this
narrative. Earlier commemoration of Anzac, for example, paid
far more attention to the strategy of the Dardanelles campaign, and to the adversaries; it was more closely keyed to the
actual conflict.

    In other words, it is the role of the historian to consider
how these pilgrimages have become normalised and ritualised
to the extent that the historical and the political dimensions of

war often remain uninterrogated. Historians in different contexts have explored the process of how collective memory becomes part of normal political ritual. Jeffrey Olick considers this in the context of German wartime commemoration where, he observes, 'the commemorative apparatus has become a rather well-oiled machine'. An acknowledgement of historical responsibility, he writes, has 'become [a] regular feature of the political liturgy'.[12] In becoming a natural part of cultural life, political challenges are lost. Emotions such as mourning and loss need to be subjected to analysis as part of the historical narrative that is being told of the pilgrimages.

Furthermore, the historian would reflect on the ways in which the tourist genre produces a ritual that normalises these events. What we see today is a new version of an old relationship between war and tourism. Robin Gerster and Peter Pierce identify the theme of tourism in the writings of soldiers who went to war. 'War and travel go together', write the editors of On the Warparth; the tour of duty is 'itself a form of travel experience'.[13] This process of normalising war through travel was undertaken by the soldiers themselves. There was criticism of those young, naive men who enthusiastically joined up to be paid to travel abroad when few could do so; they were derogatorily referred to as 'six bob a day' tourists. Since then, relatives of those who perished have, from time to time, visited the battlefield, but it was with the 50th anniversary in 1965 that Australians returned in significant numbers. They were greeted by about a hundred people, writes Ken Inglis, among them four Australian hitch-hikers, 'unexpected evidence that some young Australians cared about the Anzac tradition'.[14] This trip involved 300 pilgrims and it helped to establish the new ritual. A distinctive element in this 1965 tour of the battlefield was the acceptance by the Turkish government and people of the visits, and they continue to encourage such tourism. The industry that now surrounds Anzac tours has been a great boon for tourism in Turkey; as Wright observed, '[c]ompetition in the Anzac trade . . . was fierce'.[15] Almost forty years after the 1965 trek, the numbers of visitors continue to increase each year and the phenomenon of the pilgrimage has taken a very different course. Wright describes the setting for remembrance:

> I scrambled up from the beach and discovered there wasn't a square centimetre of lawn that wasn't occupied. Thousands of bodies lay side by side in sleeping bags. Small groups sat around, singing and laughing and yelling to each other. Pretty obviously, all these people had arrived during the day to secure prime positions. Above the lawn, thousands more figures moved around in the darkness, lit weirdly by large spotlights, and buses continued crawling along the road.[16]

Wright creates a domesticated image, one that is ordinary and mundane as people gather to remember. 'Tour guides were setting up chairs for their older customers in a natural bowl, and families and school groups were burrowing into the undergrowth to gain a bit of territory.'[17] Wright evokes how the emotional and the national come together in this celebration of human spirit:

> The ceremony ended, but almost no one moved. Tom's friend Kate was weeping and the boys were clearing their throats. Tom admitted he was a 'bit shaky' and Chris volunteered that he had discovered a tear in his eye . . . Ben, usually slow to display any emotion blurted out: 'I've been fighting back the tears for ten minutes. I found it all amazing. I've never felt so proud to be Australian.'[18]

He describes how crowds gathered around cemeteries of fallen soldiers, draped in flags:

> A sizeable crowd had built at Lone Pine . . . Within the cemetery itself was an even bigger gathering. Thousands of people, almost all of them young, had taken possession of the rows of graves. Every gravestone had at least three young people standing or sitting around it. Some youngsters had draped Australian flags over the

stones. More draped flags over their own shoulders, or had the flags painted on their faces. I remember a conversation around a table back at Anzac House with a group of young travellers] They were all republicans they said, but they worried that a republican leader would want to replace the Australian flag . . . It was, they declared, part of their country's history. And here at Lone Pine was proof of that attachment.[19]

In analysing these events, the historian, like the journalist, is 'bearing witness' to the emotional responses by the pilgrims to this commemorative moment. The historian not only has the task of documenting and observing this form of memory as an aesthetic exercise—as one where emotions are observed and captured—but is bound by an ethical imperative to analyse this process historically and politically. The version of history presented through these commemorative impulses, a historian might observe, can never be an absolute truth of the past; it can only be a representation of it. Commemorations are ever-changing, political and social constructs. As John Gillis notes, 'they have no existence beyond our politics, our social relations and our histories'.[20] In other words, for the historian, these memories need to be understood as *contested*.

The question of amnesia is central to a historian's task, as what is forgotten is of course as important as what is remembered. The ethics of history alerts us to the ways in which contemporary concerns shape our historical understandings, and thus there can be no absolute truth about how an event should or can be interpreted, remembered or understood. We view the past through the lens of the present and so each generation has a different way of reading its history. The most significant shift in remembrance of Anzac Day has been the remarkable move from a critique of what it symbolised for the generation immediately after the war to an embracing of it by the present generation of young backpackers. The shift in perception and meaning of Anzac Day has been remarkable: while the generation immediately after World War II was critical of it and of what it symbolised, the present generation of young backpackers embraces it. They recall youthful loss and heroism, with no apparent or explicit valorisation of war; but the events commemorated by Anzac Day are no longer as heavily contested as they have been in the past.

The Vietnam generation condemned the wartime activities of their elders and Anzac Day symbolised those activities. They dramatised war, questioned its purpose and offered various analyses of how and why it emerged. Their emotion was evident in their analyses: they were angry with their elders for condemning young men to a futile war and then idealising it. The most celebrated text, which reflects this view is the 1959 play, *The One Day of the Year*, by Alan Seymour where Anzac Day is associated with the indulgences of a generation of drunken larrikin veterans. In the minds of the vociferous critics in the play, war is to be loudly denunciated not domesticated and given legitimacy through a ritualisation process. Hughie Cook, a university student and son of Alf Cook, a digger, serves as a mouthpiece for his generation when he denounces his father's romancing of Anzac Day. Hughie sums up his frustration when he confides to Jan, a fellow student with whom he is writing an article on Anzac Day for the university paper: 'Anzac. Gallipoli! God, there's been another war since then. Dozens of wars everywhere, thousands of lousy little victories and defeats. But they go on and on about this one as though it was the greatest thing, war or peace, that ever happened to this country.'[21] Determined to finally challenge the Anzac discourse that dominated his childhood, Hughie declares 'that old eyewash about national character's a thing of the past . . . Australians make the greatest soldiers, the best fighters, it's all rubbish'.[22] When questioned on his knowledge of the battle he retorts: 'The official history, all very glowing and patriotic . . . Do you know what that Gallipoli campaign meant? Bugger all'.[23] Alf replies to his son's representation of Australian diggers as drunks and larrikins:

You can't see past a few drinks. You can't. Is that all you saw the other day? . . . All right, said it couldn't never be a victory. They lost. But they'd tried. They tried and they was beaten. A man's not too bad who'll stand up in the street and remember when he was licked. Ay?[24]

In another forum, this critique of Anzac Day was also dramatically played out in the campaigns by Women Against Rape in War who marched on Anzac Day to reclaim the experience of all women in war. In declaring it a 'day of mourning', feminists wished to raise the general issue of 'rape and sexual politics, of war, male violence and militarism'. They sought 'recognition of the violence perpetrated on women in all wars and to bring the reality of war—every war—to the fore'.[25] Through these activities and those of left-wing groups, there was a resistance to normalise war and make it a natural and uncontested part of Australian identity. In the transition from anger to idealisation of Anzac mythology by Australia's youth, we have turned full circle. For those in the 1960s and 1970s, Anzac Day became the rallying point of opposition against the futility of war and male violence in war. In the early twenty-first century, it is focal point in the search for community by a white society that lacks myth and ritual. Each interpretation emerges from the preoccupations of the era from which it emerges; in these shifting sands the historian's role is to identify the contested nature of these memories when these elements have dropped away.

The past, argues Alvin Rosenfield, 'is never permanently fixed but rather shifts in contour and meaning with the changing shapes of symbolisation and interpretation'.[26] The ethics in- volved in writing history requires capturing and understand- ing this moving feast through analysis without losing empathy for the motives, intentions, experiences and the subjectivity of historical actors. This includes an analysis of emotions in history and how these have been played out in acts of memory. Reflecting on the ways in which the Anzac myth has been negotiated tells us much about how the expression of emotions, sentiment and ritualisation by each generation can interpret a traumatic event differently. The historian acts as society's conscience not to forget what Lacquer describes as an appreciation of 'the history of the political and moral failures' that so tragically led our men to the slaughter. Without this analysis we are left with little or no sense of ethics or history and no better understanding of the treacherous acts of war, of our world, or of ourselves.

NOTES

[1]   Thomas Laqueur, 'The sound of voices: Intoning names', *London Review of Books*, 5 June 1997, p. 3.

[2]   Daniel Abramson, 'Make history, not memory', *Harvard Design Magazine*, Fall, no. 9, 1999, p. 2.

[3]   Saul Friedlander, 'History, memory, and the historian: Facing the Shoah', in Michael S. Roth and Charles G. Salas (eds), *Disturbing Remains: Memory, History, and Crisis in the Twentieth Century*, Getty Research Institute, Los Angeles, 2001, pp. 277–9.

[4]   Laqueur, p. 3.

[5]   R. G. Collingwood, *The Idea of History*, Clarendon Press, Oxford, 1946, p. 304.

[6]   See Barbara H. Rosenwein, 'Worrying about emotions in history', *American Historical Review*, June 2002, pp. 821–45.

[7]   Michael S. Roth and Charles G. Salas, 'Introduction', in Roth and Salas (eds), *Disturbing Remains*, p. 2.

[8]   Michelle Griffin, 'Pilgrims' progress', *Age*, 24 April 2004, Review, p. 8.

[9]   Lyn Spillman, 'When do collective memories last?: Founding moments in the United States and Australia', in Jeffrey K. Olick (ed.), *States of Memory: Continuities, Conflicts, and Transformations in National Retrospection*, Duke University Press, Durham, NC, 2003. For a recent discussion of the Anzac mythology, see Graham Seal,

Inventing Anzac: the Digger and National Mythology, University of Queensland Press, Brisbane, 2004, p. 4.

10 Bruce Scates, 'In Gallipoli's shadow: Pilgrimage, memory, mourning and the Great War', *Australian Historical Studies*, vol. 33, no. 119, April, 2002, pp. 1–21.

11 Tony Wright, *Turn Right at Istanbul: A Walk on the Gallipoli Peninsula*, Allen & Unwin, Sydney, 2003, p. 215.

12 Jeffrey K. Olick, 'What does it mean to normalise the past?: Official memory in German politics since 1989', in Olick (ed.), *States of Memory*, p. 265.

13 Robin Gerster and Peter Pierce (eds), *On the Warpath: An Anthology of Australian Military Travel*, Melbourne University Press, Melbourne, 2004, p. 1.

14 K. S. Inglis, 'Gallipoli pilgrimage—1965', in Gerster and Pierce (eds), *On the Warpath*, p. 287.

15 Wright, p. 113.

16 Wright, p. 209.

17 Wright, p. 210.

18 Wright, p. 223.

19 Wright., pp. 218–19.

20 John R. Gillis (ed.), *Commemorations: The Politics of National Identity*, Princeton University Press, Princeton, 1944, p. 5.

21 Alan Seymour, *The One Day of the Year*, in *Three Australian Plays*, Penguin, Melbourne, 1985, p. 38.

22 Seymour, p. 42

23 Seymour, p. 79.

24 Seymour, p. 86.

25 Adrian Howe, 'Anzac mythology and the feminist challenge', Critiques of Australian Society, *Melbourne Journal of Politics*, vol. 15, 1983–84, pp. 17–18.

26 Alvin Rosenfeld, 'Popularisation and memory: The case of Anne Frank', in Peter Hayes (ed.), *Lessons and Legacies: The Meaning of the Holocaust in a Changing World*, Northwestern University Press, Evanston, Ill., 1991, p. 277.

CHAPTER 3

GREG DENING

LIVING WITH AND IN DEEP TIME

I was honoured a few years ago by being invited by the National Library of Australia to celebrate the entry of two items of our Australian heritage in the Memory of the World register. The Memory of the World register identifies objects and documents, which, while having special importance at the local and national level, also have their place in the whole world's history. The Magna Carta, the US Declaration of Independence and the Rosetta Stone would be examples. The two Australian documents deemed as important as the like of these in world history are Captain James Cook's own journal of his *Endeavour* voyage of discovery in 1768–71, and the Edward Mabo Papers, a huge collection of the documents from the Mabo Case on indigenous people's land rights in the High Court of Australia.

Cook's *Endeavour* Journal (MS 1, Manuscript One) is in sentiment and fact the foundation document of our National Library, established as the Parliamentary Library at the time of federation. It is in Cook's own hand with his errors and corrections and afterthoughts. New ~~Whales~~, he writes as his name for his discoveries on the east coast of Australia. He crosses that out for ~~New Wales~~ and crosses that out for New South Wales.

I don't mind confessing that I, who have read many times Professor J. C. Beaglehole's transcript of this journal in the Hakluyt Society edition of Cook's journals, found it an entirely different experience to turn the pages of the original. I count it as one of the true privileges of a historian to read the pages men and women write fresh from some experience. Their pens sometimes tremble with emotion, or they write with a flourish their first thoughts on what they are experiencing. I travel the world to read these thousands of pages—journals, diaries, letters, and scribbled notes. I have an obligation of a lifetime towards archivists and librarians who have served me, towards citizens of all countries who support their institutions of memory, towards the taxpayers and their governments who fund these institutions. Thank you, I say to them all. You have given me years of pleasure and a richness of life more than I can say.

So when MS 1 is brought in on its special trolley from the safe in the National Library's Manuscript Reading Room, I am sitting nervously with my white cotton gloves on. I have a fistful of pencils all sharpened at my side. No pens allowed in this room. And if you have ever had the excruciating experience of sharpening a pencil in the silence of this room, you will come with several already sharpened.

MS 1 is a manuscript you read very slowly, savouring every mark and scratching on the page. You know where these pages were written, in Cook's tiny cabin on the port side of the Endeavour's Great Cabin. The National Library even has the small portable desk on which it was written. You will have to imagine the ship's movement and the smell of hemp, tar and the fug of humanity. The Great Cabin outside is packed with clubs, statues and feathered robes from Tahiti and Aotearoa

(New Zealand). The artist, Sydney Parkinson, is drawing the plants and animals that Joseph Banks had collected. Maybe Tupaia, the Tahitian priest whom Banks is taking home to England as part of his collection, is drawing his map of all the islands his people know and have visited in the Pacific long before Cook's 'discovery' of them. Turn the pages of MS 1 you will find Cook despondent on the worst day of his life when he had killed a Maori with his own hand. Or he is sitting there musing on the difficulties of being a discoverer. He is there minutes after looking with horror at the chasm of a wave re-coilling from the coral wall of the Great Barrier Reef. He had taken the *Endeavour* within a few hundred feet of destruction.

This voyage of Cook all the way up the Australian coast from Point Hicks to Cape York is perhaps the most remarkable voyage of discovery of all time. All our lives have been affected by it. It certainly belongs to the Memory of the World.

The Mabo Papers are another sort of experience for a historian. Slow reading of them would take a lifetime. They are in dozens of archive boxes. They look daunting on their trolley even a few at a time. But go to an archive anywhere in the world and you will see historians sitting beside trolleys piled high with boxes. Once begun on a search, there is no ending till you are satisfied that you have seen all that there is to be seen. Sir Keith Hancock used to tell the story of the time he began researching his official history of World War II. The archives, he was told, were in aircraft hangers in the south of England. The first thing he did was to buy a bicycle so he could ride the miles of shelving. Yes, it is also the historian's task to read fast, exhaustively, to digest massive quantities of data and to have the correct note-taking system that records what she or he has read accurately and will allow others to go where the historian has been. 'Being there', which gives an anthropologist authority to describe a culture, is for historians that feeling for the past that can only be matched by the hours, the days, the months, the years she or he sits at the desks of the archives. It is the assurance that one's extravagance with time there is rewarded with a sensitivity that comes in no other way. It is an overlaying of images one on another. It is a realisation that knowledge of the past is cumulative, kaleidoscopic, and extravagantly wasteful of time and energy.

There is one file in the Mabo Papers that you will certainly need cotton gloves for, and needs a slow, slow read. It is the file with Eddie Mabo's drawings of the land of his island people, its boundaries, and its names, the memories imprinted on it. It is his expression of how deep time has left its mark on the present. How deep that deep time is we don't know. But we know that the land on which Eddie Mabo lives has been lived on for more than forty thousand years. Mabo's knowledge of his land comes to him through story, dance, ritual, legend, myth and his own life experiences of conflict and family loyalties. He taps a truth the way we all tap truths from living, but in ways which need to be tolerated by those whose notion of law and evidence is blinkered by legal tradition and constitution and who need to find some entry into Eddie Mabo's otherness. The other papers in the Mabo Papers—of judges, lawyers, anthropologists, historians, witnesses of first people telling their stories—belong to the Memory of the World because the whole world faces the issue of how it lives with the Deep Time of all its first peoples, overrun and dispossessed as they are. It belongs to World Memory because the papers are we, the Australian people, struggling to do justice and to live with the Deep Time all around us. And we are in this instance the world.

Fifty years ago I made a discovery that changed my life. I discovered that I wanted to write the history of the 'other side of the beach', of indigenous Pacific island peoples and Australian first peoples. I had no cultural bound with them. They would be my 'Natives'. And on 'this side of the beach', my side as an outsider, as 'Stranger', I wanted to write the history of people whom the world deemed 'little'. I wanted to write history from below. Not of kings and queens. Not of writers of constitutions and saviours of nations. 'Little people'. Those on whom the forces of the world press most hardly. I wanted to celebrate their humanity, their freedom, their creativity, the way they crossed the boundaries around their lives.

This is a hard history to write. Neither 'natives' nor 'little people' leave much of their past. I thought I needed a special reading skill to read what was absent in the records and to hear the silences. I thought that that reading skill was anthropology. So I went to Harvard to do my doctorate in anthropology, the better to write the history I wanted to write.

I didn't go to anthropology to get out of history. My mind had been blown by the history I had done as an undergraduate at the University of Melbourne. R. H. Tawney, Max Weber, R. G. Collingwood, Marc Bloch, Thucydides have left their mark on my life ever since. I moved to the marginal areas of historical inquiry, where history is blended with archaeology, linguistics and mythology. Sutton Hoo, the extraordinary Anglo-Saxon burial, had just been discovered. I flew in my mind with O. G. S. Crawford at sunset and sunrise in his 'tiger moth' over the wheat and barley fields of England and saw the shadows of villages lost in the Black Death. I travelled the Silk Road. I puzzled over ancient Greek pottery in India. I went with the founding father of modern Australian archaeology, John Mulvaney, on his dig at Fromm's Landing near Mannum on the Murray River. I watched him hold in his hands the micro stone artefacts that were left after four thousand years occupation of the site. But I knew that he would write his history of those four thousand years out of the pollen, the seeds, and the bones that we had dug up.

In Oceania—the Australasian/Pacific region Mulvaney was introducing us students to—the intellectual puzzle was how to describe a past when all of time was on the surface of things—in the typology of artefacts, in glottochronology—the study of the age and origins of language, in the genetics of blood groups, in the ethnobotany (other cultural categorisations) of plants. Time is the sections of a fish's ear bone; time is the rings of growth of a tree; time is a pollen count; time is the character of sands in a dune.

Knowledge of this sort is hard won, full of debates and counter-claims, zigzagging through a dozen disciplines. It is never static. There are no short cuts. It is self-interested—in personal ambitions, in institutional rivalries, in the scramble for funded support. But altruism and idealism suffuse it too. There is a passion that such knowledge be public, that it be subject to critical appraisal, that it serve a good that is greater than an individual's fame. It was a brilliant time for a young scholar, as if life were a Times Literary Crossword Puzzle. We felt that the past belonged to us because we had the skills to discover it.

Fifty years on, I now know that to be wrong. The past belongs to those on whom it impinges, and they will represent it in many different ways. They dance it. They sing it. They paint it. They play it.

The first realisation that the past belongs to those on whom it impinges rather than those who have the skill to discover it came like a kick in the stomach. In 1960, Frantz Fanon published *The Wretched of the Earth*. In a world of victims of colonisation, he wrote, there are no innocents. No one can write two-sided history who in some way benefits by the power of victors. No one can mediate between the dispossessed living and the voiceless dead. Suddenly we 'Strangers' felt intruders in writing about the victimised cultures of our first peoples. At conferences and seminars indigenous scholars attacked us. How could we know their past? They asked. How could we speak for them? These were hard times. We each had our own answer. I can't give life to the dead or justice to the victims in the past. But I am with Karl Marx. The function of my history is not just to understand the world. It is also to change it. If my history by story or reflection disturbs the moral lethargy of the present, then it fulfils a need. I haven't silenced any one's voice by adding mine. It was at this time that we began, whenever we spoke of First People—here in Australia, in the Pacific, in the Americas—to honour them in their past whenever we began to speak of them. It is not much, but sometimes these things work by cultural osmosis. Recently in a ceremony of naturalisation of citizens, the City of Boroondara flew the Aboriginal flag as well as the Australian flag, and honoured the first people of the land before everything else.

James Cook ended his voyage up the east coast on 'Posession Island'—his spelling in MS 1. Possession Island is an island in Torres Straits to the west of Cape York. Cook takes possession there in the name of King George III of all he had 'discovered' on the east coast. There are all sorts of ways of taking possession —turning soil, leaving plaques, saying mass, leaving coins in a bottle. Cook did it by climbing to the top of the hill of the island, raising a flag, giving a musket and cannon salute, and three British cheers.

Cook was more worried by the Dutch at this moment. But he noted that all the way up the coast, wherever he landed, the people defended themselves and their land. He noted in his journal how these people seemed perfectly happy with their lot and were not in the least interested in anything the civilised had to offer them. He did not see any signs of how these people used their land, but then he could not have known that the fires that he had seen first near Batemans Bay and then all up the coast, were not camp fires, but the way the first people cleared their land and managed it. Of course, he experiences the first people's other uses of fire at Endeavour

River, when they tried to burn the *Endeavour* off the land. His crew presumed that everything in the sea and river was theirs to catch. It didn't occur to them that the turtles and the fish belonged to somebody very particularly. They were being punished for stealing as they had punished every first people on their voyage for stealing. I suppose it is a small irony that almost twenty years later Botany Bay and Port Jackson would be settled by many people who were being punished for stealing.

Cook when he was approaching Possession Island saw first people on the beach preparing to defend their land. He noticed something different. For the first time he saw among their weapons bows and arrows. These were Torres Straits islanders. It is another nice irony. At the very moment of their dispossession, Eddie Mabo's ancestors were there protesting their loss.

We all live in deep time. All of us alive are equally distant from our human beginnings through the generations, through the millennia, through the eons of evolution. But deep time impinges on us differently. The deep time reaching back to Jesus Christ makes me, a Christian, differently from the way deep time reaching back to Muhammad makes a Muslim, or Buddha a Buddhist. In a period of 'discovery', encounter, settlement, colony and post-colony, deep time impinges differently on those who were there first and those who came later to the land.

Our more shallow time of two hundred years and more impinges closely on us. James Cook's story, Ned Kelly's, the Eureka Stockade, the convict settlement, Gallipoli, the Kokoda Trail—we see ourselves in the histories we make of these events. We see our humanistic, altruistic selves in Cook's voyages of scientific discovery. We see the courage we want to have in those who had it aplenty. We see the larrikin element in our fight for justice. We own our pasts and ourselves in them.

We live beside and are bound together forever with a people who feel that their Deep Time impinges as closely on them as our shallow time impinges on us. The sort of history we make of this bound-together state will need to be as generous, as humane, and as imaginative as it is exhaustive, careful, cumulative and kaleidoscopic. But is there any other way history should be written?

CHAPTER 4

GRAEME DAVISON

A HISTORIAN IN THE MUSEUM: THE ETHICS OF PUBLIC HISTORY

Museum politics have recently captured the headlines in Australia as they have in several western democracies. Everywhere, it seems, people are debating what historical museums should show, how their exhibitions should be interpreted, and who should decide. Often the contest is between historians, or curators with historical training, on the one hand, and governments, museum boards and other stakeholders, on the other. The most intense of these controversies pit liberals or progressives against cultural conservatives. Critics often accuse museum curators and historians of being 'politically correct' members of the 'new class', while the critics, in turn, are labelled as 'neocons' and patriotic reactionaries.

Over the past five years or so, as a historical advisor to the National Museum of Australia, I have been a close observer of how these conflicts have been played out in one of our main cultural institutions. During that time, I was invited by the director and council to attempt to resolve contested issues of historical interpretation: I reviewed the labels for exhibits, drew up guidelines for the selection and interpretation of 'content', and, at a crucial moment, responded to the attacks on the museum's interpretation of Australian history by a discontented member of its own council, David Barnett, who was believed to have close links to the Prime Minister. Most of these tasks were undertaken in the months approaching the opening of the new museum building on Acton Peninsula, long after the exhibition briefs had been decided and fabrication was well under way. It was a modest role though enough to somehow persuade one of the museum's critics that I was its 'intellectual architect' and author of its 'post-modern' approach to historical interpretation![1]

Advising public institutions on politically sensitive issues, especially when you can't control the outcome, is the kind of work that more sensible historians would probably avoid. Over the years, first as a chair of the Victorian Historic Buildings Council, and later in advising the National Museum of Australia (NMA), I have often found myself pondering the distinctive ethical and political dilemmas that arise for the historian who acts, not as author of their own interpretation of the past, but as an advisor to a public institution serving the wider community. Current approaches to heritage, for example, often suggest that conservation of buildings and historic landscapes should reflect community values as well as expert opinion.[2] Museum interpretations of the national past, like the programs of a national broadcaster, are also expected to reflect some kind of 'balance' of community opinion. But how does the historian give advice when the community itself is divided? Where does expertise end and politics begin?[3] What weight should be given to 'community opinion' if it differs from the scholarly consensus? In this essay I reflect on how these issues are being worked out in national museums, and defend the pluralist approach that I sought to uphold in my own advisory role at the NMA.[4]

Recent ructions at the NMA echo similar controversies in American and British museums. In 1994 American historians and museum curators clashed with Air Force veterans and conservative politicians when the Smithsonian's Air and Space Museum in Washington proposed to install the *Enola Gay*, the aeroplane that dropped the first atomic bomb on Hiroshima, as the centrepiece of a special commemorative exhibit. The question that caused most conflict was whether the exhibit should show the devastating effects of the bomb on the Japanese people as well as telling the story of the American aircrew and their role in bringing the war to an end.[5] In this encounter, the conservatives won a pyrrhic victory when plans for the exhibition were scrapped and the director of the Air and Space Museum, who had defended a 'balanced' interpretation, resigned. More recently, the liberals won back a little ground when the proposal of a conservative businesswoman, Mrs Catherine Reynolds, to endow the Smithsonian Institution's Museum of American History with a 'Gallery of American Achievers', designed by her own hand-picked committee, was overturned by opposition from academics and newspapers.[6] In Britain, meanwhile, conservative newspapers have attacked 'post-colonial' exhibits on the history of slavery at the National Maritime Museum while applauding the more 'balanced' approach of the new, privately funded British Empire and Commonwealth Museum in Bristol.[7] Even in continental Europe, which long seemed immune from the fractious cultural politics of the Anglo-democracies, controversy has recently erupted over the interpretation of colonial history in Belgian and French museums.

For centuries museums were synonymous with dry-as-dust history, so why have their activities now become so politically charged?

Museums now enjoy high public regard as influential and authoritative sources of national history. When people in Australia and the United States are asked to rank the sources of information about the past that they trust, museums come close to the top of the poll, well ahead of history teachers, and far ahead of politicians, who come last.[8] Why citizens place such confidence in museums as a source of information about their history, and less in other sources, such as teachers, is less clear. Perhaps it's the reassuring appearance of reliability that comes from a tangible, rather than a discursive, past. Because museums are so trusted, and visited by large numbers of school-children on compulsory excursions, their interpretations of the national past are also likely to be scrutinised more intently by those who fear that the nation's youth may be led astray.

Public interest in museums appears to have grown along with mounting concern about globalisation, illegal migration, terrorism and other threats to the integrity of the nation state. When the nation is under siege, it is natural to seek to shore up its defences, cultural as well as military. This has been one of the preoccupations of conservative supporters of both the Bush and Howard governments. One of the effects of global change, as Judith Brett observes, is to polarise the per-spectives of 'cosmopolitans'—intellectuals and others skilled in speculative inquiry, who welcome the opportunities for cross-cultural encounters—and 'locals'—those who seek refuge in familiar experiences and traditional values. The national museum has become a lightning rod for such conflicts.[9]

Finally, controversy grows more intense for lack of an agreed framework for resolving differences. On one view, these disagreements are essentially political and irreconcilable. Museums are caught in the crossfire of the wider culture wars; all they can do is to lie low and hope to duck the flak. This is a cynical view that I have struggled to resist. I came to the discussions at the NMA with the hope that if museum pro-fessionals, historians and council members had a clearer under-standing of their roles, and of the respective contributions of historical expertise and lay opinion, many of these differences could be ameliorated, if not overcome. When the conflicts between members of the museum's council and curators were at their most intense, my fellow historical advisors and I argued that the role of the council was to establish guidelines for exhibitions and to leave the detailed execution of the policy to the museum's staff. When I was invited by the museum to draft some guidelines, I was hopeful of arriving at a consensus that would permit the council to have its say while leaving the creative energies of the curatorial staff unfettered.

The guidelines I proposed reflected a pluralistic philosophy of the museum as a house of many mansions. I did not invent this philosophy myself, but sought to distil the principles that had guided the museum since Geoffrey Blainey and John Mulvaney wrote its charter in the 1974 Piggott Report. Its spirit is well expressed in the following summary under the heading 'About Us' on the NMA's website:

> The National Museum of Australia explores the land, nation and people of Australia.
>
> The Museum celebrates Australian social history in a unique way by revealing the stories of ordinary and extraordinary Australians, promoting the exploration of knowledge and ideas and providing a dynamic forum for discussion and reflection.
>
> With a history of challenging convention and encouraging debate about who we are as Australians and what shapes our national culture and psyche, the Museum is sometimes controversial and never dull. For every Australian visitor, there is something to remember, share, enjoy or learn. For overseas visitors, there is the chance to experience, through sight, sound and touch, what Australia used to be, what it is now and what it could be, motivating them to travel further in Australia, having had a taste of a living, dynamic and futuristic museum.

Arriving at agreement on the guidelines took several months of vigorous discussion between the historical advisors and council members, especially over the balance that the

museum was expected to strike between patriotic and inspir-
ational themes, on the one hand, and critical or 'challenging'
ones, on the other. (The word 'challenging' especially troubled
the conservative members of the NMA council, one of whom
told me that it was a 'new class' code-word for 'subversive
of legitimate authority'!). When the guidelines were finally
agreed in a version that seemed to meet the expectations of
everyone, however, it did almost nothing to produce the consensus I had hoped for. Perhaps this was because the guidelines
were simply too generalised to be useful. Perhaps it was because
balance, after all, is very much in the eye of the beholder. (In
the midst of the debate the *Australian* had described me as a
'middle of the road historian', a title I could wear with equa-
nimity, if not with pride. By the end of the affair, I observed—
to another newspaper—that there now seemed to be rather
more lanes on my right than when I'd set out.) However, the
main reason that we failed, I believe, was that the museum's
critics were not really pluralists at heart. For them, the issues
were not finally about scholarly expertise, or balance, but
about whether the museum reflected the right political values.

There are now probably more historians employed in public
institutions as museum curators, heritage professionals, archivists
and the like than there are in the universities, and the terms on
which they are employed have a vital bearing on the interpretation of the national past. The ethical standards they developed
as historians within the academy have now to be negotiated
within institutions with their own political and bureaucratic
imperatives.[10] It may help to clarify the choices before us if we
consider three institutional models of how museums engage
with their publics, especially in dealing with morally or politically contentious subjects.

In the first, which I call 'the authorised version', the government selects the story to be told and the historians carry out

the government's orders. The museum deals with contested issues by imposing its own version.

There are many examples around the world, though fewer than there were, of museums built along these lines. I recall visiting a museum in Leningrad in the mid-1960s, when the long shadow of Stalin had only just begun to lift from Soviet life. The highlight, an exhibit on the history of the city's long siege by the Nazis during World War II, climaxed with a documentary film of the celebrations after relief of the city. The footage had been shot from the front of a slowly moving vehicle as it progressed through crowds celebrating their deliverance, and waving at the obviously adored occupant of the vehicle whose image, however, had now been mysteriously expunged from the show. De-Stalinisation, in the museum context, meant simply running the movie as before, with the shots of Stalin, the great patriotic leader, now chopped out. Such authorised versions of the national past may be fascinating to the historian, though more for what they reveal about their creators than their subject. They are exactly the kinds of museums that ought to be in a museum.

Some western conservatives now seem to yearn for the kind of unified national spirit that they observe in more authoritarian regimes, a yearning that grows as the democracies feel themselves under threat, whether from terrorism or cultural fragmentation. Perhaps this is why museums are in the sights of neo-conservatives in the United States and their followers in Australia. In the United States Mrs Lynn Cheney, wife of the Vice President, has accused national cultural institutions, including museums, of failing to offer America's youth a sufficiently inspiriting and unifying version of its past.[11] John Carroll, chair of the recent NMA committee of review, entitles his most recent book *The Western Dreaming: The western world is dying for want of a story*. He yearns for a similar inspiring national story in the exhibitions and public programs of the NMA. While his report clears the museum of 'systemic bias'— so confirming my own previous advice to its council—his call for a unified narrative organised around heroic figures and iconic objects clearly departs from the pluralism of the museum's recent practice. Even if the West lacks a story, I'm not sure that conservatives should assume the right to supply one for everyone else. We are still, thankfully, far from enacting such a model at the NMA, or any other Australian museum. But when a review of a national museum is directed to report on whether its exhibitions and public programs had realised the 'vision' of the government, it is already well on the way towards authorising its own version of the national past.[12]

In the second model, which I call 'institutional consensus', the museum's council and staff together establish the framework for their public exhibitions. There may be energetic discussion and criticism in the process of developing this consensus, but all the fights occur in-house. While the government may influence the framework through its appointments to the museum's council, the historians and other professional staff retain some creative freedom in deciding how that consensus is expressed.

This is the way most state-sponsored museums actually operate. The appointment of councils at arm's length from governments is supposed to ensure that policy is framed by people with relevant expertise and a range of views. However, recently governments in Australia have shown a tendency to make appointments on political criteria, and to demand a higher level of accountability, both financially and politically. Being myself among the last living nineteenth-century liberals (and therefore an admirable specimen for a museum), I believe that the composition of councils ought to reflect a wide range of political views and relevant professional skills. Such a perspective is probably now out of favour with politicians and bureaucrats.

The trouble with the idea of institutional consensus is that it inevitably tends towards the lowest common denominator. Whatever is unobjectionable to everyone is very likely to excite no one. You can walk through some museums and easily reconstruct the deliberations of the committees that created them. All the 'stakeholders' have been consulted, all the relevant government policies have been observed, all the important interest groups have been represented: the result, all too often, is bland and boring. The museum becomes bureaucratised, creative initiative is fettered, and people mind their backs instead of the interests of the public. The tensions that everyone knows are present in the nation's history are suppressed rather than being themselves made a subject of inquiry and display. Too often managerial imperatives become the excuse for whiting out, or dumbing down, initiatives that may make waves with the politicians or top bureaucrats.

In the third model—the one I call 'civic pluralism'—the museum acts as a broad church, hospitable to a range of interpretative viewpoints. The museum presents itself to visitors as a forum, a place for civic discourse. Or it could be likened to a production house that hosts many different creative people and teams. Curatorial staff would be appointed to work as teams, much like the creative teams who make films, to develop exhibits that express their own interpretations of the national past and contemporary culture, and to meet community interests and expectations. In the pluralist model, interpretative differences are not suppressed, as they are by the authorised version, or submerged, as in the institutional consensus; instead they are encouraged and made part of the show. While the first two models implicitly treat visitors as children, unable to think for themselves, the pluralist model invites visitors to share the excitement and tension of thinking about the nation's past and future for themselves.

The pluralist model encounters a number of criticisms. Conservatives often accuse its advocates of cultural relativism. (This seemed to be the thrust of Windschuttle's attack on my role as an advisor to the NMA when he accused me of being the 'architect' of its postmodernist philosophy.) Since I am not actually a cultural relativist or a postmodernist, my support for interpretative pluralism may require a brief word of explanation. While I don't believe that historical truth is entirely contingent, I do recognise, as a matter of everyday experience, that scholars and citizens, even when they are well informed and disinterested, disagree about important aspects of the national past. These differences are sometimes about the facts, sometimes about which facts are most relevant, sometimes about how the facts should be valued. I hold to pluralism as a working philosophy for public institutions not because I believe, when I write history myself, that truth is impossible, or that you can have any version of history you like; but because I respect these honestly held differences of interpretation and because I don't believe that you should to use public money to give an institutional imprimatur to any particular version. The accusation of moral or cultural relativism, as Don Watson rightly observes, is part of the scare tactics of conservatives seeking to impose their own frightening kind of 'moral clarity'.[13]

Some critics argue that in practice pluralism means using public funds to subsidise the self-indulgence of the most avant-garde, obscure, politically correct forms of cultural production. Museums, like universities and public broadcasters, they say, have become captive to the 'new class', the intellectual descendants of the discredited pro-communist Left. These apparatchiks have set about creating jobs for each other in such remunerative new enterprises as 'the land rights industry', and 'the guilt industry'.[14] Though I have caricatured this view, just a bit, I believe that it raises an important point for those of us who uphold the pluralist approach. How does the museum, or broadcasting service or university, ensure that the diversity of views it says it stands for is actually maintained? How does it decide where the balance of community views is to be struck? Over what period and what range of activities? And who decides?

I often asked myself similar questions as I read many hundreds of exhibition labels for the National Museum, and pondered how to respond to David Barnett's criticisms. I was wary of the possibility that the historical advisor might unconsciously become a political censor or an apologist for the museum. Sometimes I criticised labels because they were factually inaccurate, though more often because they were badly written. Sometimes the label reflected an interpretation or viewpoint that I did not hold myself; but, because it was backed by evidence and the scholarship of other historians whose work I considered sound, I noted the difference yet did not suggest that the label be changed. Where I thought the primary historical significance of an object was being ignored in order to make a tendentious or invalid point, however, I objected strenuously. When I was asked by the chair of the NMA Council to respond to the criticisms of David Barnett, I did not ask whether the labels to which he objected coincided with my own views of the subject in question; only whether they were factually accurate and 'consistent with reputable scholarship'.

Defenders of a pluralist approach to historical interpretation in museums are under an obligation to ensure that the pluralism is genuine. Exhibitions and public programs should reflect a wide range of political, social and religious viewpoints, provided always that the views expressed are based upon scholarly research and advanced within a framework of mutual respect and openness. These should include topics and themes with strong appeal to conservatives, such as ideas of national achievement, innovation, patriotic endeavour, as well as those that appeal to liberals or radicals. The job of maintaining this diversity should fall primarily to the museum's director, advised by the board and staff. The director should enjoy a degree of independence, preferably backed by statute, in carrying out his or her task. To put a museum director on a short leash, and to create a sense of insecurity around the position, as occurred during the directorship of Dawn Casey, is humiliating to the director and debilitating to the morale of the entire institution.

In every other way, however, I think that the activities of the museum should be open to much greater scrutiny than at present. I would prefer to see historians in museums define themselves as public intellectuals rather than as 'content developers', 'managers' or any of the other bureaucratic appellations they are currently expected to wear. I cannot see why the names of the authors of museum exhibits are not routinely attached to their work in labels, catalogues and websites. Is there any compelling reason why the creative work should not subjected to the same level of public scrutiny, including praise and blame, as other forms of collaborative research and interpretations, such as films or multi-author books?

I have supported this approach at every opportunity over the past few years, including in my submission to the NMA review. To my regret it has not yet attracted much support. There appears to be as much resistance to the idea from museum professionals, who prefer the safety of institutional anonymity, as there is from cultural bureaucrats who want to deny the museum's staff individual expression. Letting the public know what goes on behind the scenes, why exhibits are designed as they are, what evidence the interpreters have relied upon, is likely, on balance, to enhance respect for the work of curators as well as to raise the level of public discussion of museum interpretation. More importantly, in the current context, it is a strong affirmation of the institution's commitment to principles of professional autonomy, public accountability, free debate and genuine diversity.

To outside observers, some recent engagements in the History Wars may have seemed rather sordid. Arguments over the text of museum labels, or the footnotes in learned articles, are the kind of hand-to-hand trench warfare in which more blood often seems to be spilt than ground gained. Labels and footnotes, however, are important because they remind us that history is based, not only upon evidence, but also upon a conversation between writer and reader, historian and audience, curator and visitor. 'Only the use of footnotes enables historians to make their texts not monologues but conversations', observes Anthony Grafton in his wise and witty *The Footnote: A Curious History*. 'Wise historians know that their craft resembles Penelope's art of weaving: footnotes and text will come together again and again, in ever-changing combinations of patterns and colours. Stability is not to be reached.'[15] Beyond their diverse moral or political convictions, or their interpretations of any specific event or period, historians are united by this unending conversation between text and footnote, object and label, argument and evidence.

It's this conversation, in the last resort, that separates history from ideology or fiction. There are some Australians who are uncomfortable with the open-ended, uncertain nature of historical debate, and who yearn for the security of an authorised version of the national past. They would prefer a national museum built on iconic objects and unifying myths to one that invites its visitors to argue and talk back. It is strange that those who often praise our political freedom are so reluctant to exercise it. Our cultural institutions have already suffered much from the heavy hand of political correctness, of both left and right varieties. Perhaps it's time to reclaim them for the majority of citizens who are less interested in political orthodoxy, of either brand, than they are in enlarging our imaginations, feeding our senses, expanding our geographical and intellectual horizons and the many other goals that historical museums are uniquely able to advance.

NOTES

[1]   Keith Windschuttle, 'How not to build a museum', *Quadrant*, September 2001, pp. 11–19.; I have responded to Windschuttle's criticisms in 'Conflict in the museum' in Bain Attwood and S. G. Foster (eds), *Frontier Conflict: The Australian Experience*, National Museum of Australia, Canberra, 2003, pp. 201–14. Stuart Macintyre

reviews these events in Stuart Macintyre and Anna Clark, *History Wars*, Melbourne University Press, Melbourne, 2003, pp. 191–215.

[2] For example Denis Byrne, Helen Brayshaw and Tracy Ireland, *Social Significance: A Discussion Paper*, NSW National Parks and Wildlife Service, Sydney, 2003; Chris Johnson, *What is Social Value?*, Australian Heritage Commission, Canberra, 1994.

[3] I have commented on a parallel issue, the standing of historians as expert witnesses in court proceedings, in Graeme Davison, 'History on the witness stand: Interrogating the past', in Iain McCalman and Ann McGrath (eds), *Truth and Proof: The Humanist as Expert*, Australian Academy of Humanities 2002 Symposium Proceedings, Canberra, 2003, pp. 53–67.

[4] For earlier statements see Graeme Davison, 'National museums in a global age: Observations abroad and reflections at home', in Darryl Macintyre and Kirsten Wehner (eds), *Negotiating Histories: National Museums*, Conference Proceedings, National Museum of Australia, 2001, pp. 12–28; Graeme Davison, Submission to the Review of Exhibitions and Public Programs, National Museum of Australia, 2003 at http://www.nma.gov.au/about_us/exhibitions_and_public_programs_review/submissions/.

[5] Edward T. Linenthal and Tom Englehardt (eds), *History Wars: The Enola Gay and other Battles for the American Past*, Metropolitan Books, New York, 1996; Timothy W. Luke, 2002, *Museum Politics: Power Plays at the Exhibition*, University of Minnesota Press, Ann Arbor, MI, 2002, pp. xiii–xviii.

[6] Graeme Davison, 'Museums and the burden of national identity', *Public History Review*, no. 10, 2003, pp. 8–20.

[7] On post-colonial approaches to slavery, see Davison; for a selection of press comment on the British Empire and Commonwealth Museum see http://www.empiremuseum.co.uk/pressoffice/brilliant.htm and for an account of its approach to interpretation see Katherine Hann, 'A history of empire in a global economy', http://www.empiremuseum.co.uk/aboutus/index.htm

[8] Roy Rosenzweig, and David Thelen, *The Presence of the Past: Popular Uses of History in American Life*, Columbia University Press, New York, 1998, pp. 20–1; Paul Ashton, Jane Connors, Heather Goodall, Paula Hamilton and Louella McCarthy, 'Australians and the past at the University of Technology Sydney', *Public History Review*, vol. 8, 2000, pp. 157–67.

9   Judith Brett, *Australian Liberals and the Moral Middle Class from Alfred Deakin to John Howard*, Cambridge University Press, Melbourne, 2003, pp. 209–12.

10 I have discussed some of these issues in 'Paradigms of public history', in John Rickard and Peter Spearritt (eds), *Packaging the Past: Public Histories*, Melbourne University Press/Australian Historical Studies, Melbourne, 1991, pp. 4–15.

11 Lynne Cheney, *Telling the Truth: Why our culture and our country have stopped making sense, and what we can do about it*, Simon & Schuster, New York, 1995.

12 Terms of Reference in *Review of the National Museum of Australia, its Exhibitions and Public Programs*, NMA, Canberra, July 2003. Fortunately John Carroll and his fellow reviewers chose to interpret their terms of reference more generously than a literal reading might have suggested.

13 Don Watson, *Death Sentence: The Decay of Public Language*, Knopf, Sydney, 2003, p. 130.

14 For a discussion of this terminology see Brett, *Australian Liberals*, pp. 173–4.

15 Anthony Grafton, *The Footnote: A Curious History*, Harvard University Press, Cambridge, Mass., 1997, pp. 232–3.

CHAPTER 5

RHYS ISAAC

INCLUSIVE HISTORIES

The 'Culture Wars' that raged in the USA, and translated in Australia as the 'History Wars', should have given pause for thought to all who care about truth and understanding in public life. The attacks upon the profession have felt like an ambush sprung by those who do not themselves submit to the rigorous discipline of archival research and critical reasoning to conclusions. History for these assailants is rather a cherished legend to sustain a particular proud identity—its story is already known, independent of any enquiry. As historians recover from the shock of the hostility they have aroused, they would all do well not just to think of the politics made of the matter but also to remind themselves and the public of the road travelled that had made academic history vulnerable to the ambush.

Here I shall take up this challenge by reflecting on the reshaping of the field that has taken place in my own career lifetime, and the ethical considerations that have directed my own work.

Massive changes have occurred in the time since I was an undergraduate in the late 1950s. The basic rules of conduct have remained as they had been for some generations before I commenced my studies. Researchers had long been required to consult all the relevant documents, and to show how the history they wrote was developed out of critical reasoning from those documents—which had to be cited in precise footnotes and bibliographies. While evidentiary procedures have remained constant, wave upon wave of tumultuous events in the world have profoundly altered perceptions, so that a powerful set of democratising moral reassessments have comprehensively reshaped historiography. If the new ideals had to be summed up in a sentence, it might read 'History is to strive to be the history of everybody—female as well as male, with all races and ethnicities equally included.'

Important new choices were already beginning to be made in 1957 when, as a 19-year-old at the University of Cape Town in South Africa, I studied 'History II—Colonial Expansion', as taught by Leonard Thompson (before his distinguished career at Yale University). A new historiographic ethic was expressed in that course. If I were to speculate about its sources in that time, I would guess that the then recent grim revelations of racism run riot in the horrors of the Holocaust on the one hand, and the positive affirmations of the United Nations' 'Declaration of Universal Human Rights' on the other hand, had unsettled the old racially partisan white man's historiography. Be that as it may, Leonard Thompson's lectures fostered a strong consciousness of the histories of empire and settlement as two-sided—not just to be told as the admirable triumph of the self-declared 'civilising' settlers.

Looking back now, grateful for that awakening overview, I realise that the positive lesson was unfortunately limited by the fact that there were as yet almost no histories written about 'the other side of the frontier' to which our enlightened lecturer could send us for further reading. I realise also that it was a moral choice—an urge to help make those other histories—

that directed my teacher's and my own and many of my contemporaries' steps into historical research.

That choice began to be explicitly exercised here in Australia. It happened in the same time that I was both finding my
feet as a professional historian and settling into being an Australian, a parent of young native-born offspring. Furthermore,
it happened in an informal collaboration with two other
Australian historians—Greg Dening and Inga Clendinnen. We
were none of us then aspiring to write histories of Australia
(though Greg already had a lot of note-cards on Captain
Cook); but we were all writing histories of colonisation. We
never discussed our work and aspirations in the terms I am
now employing, but we knew that we were looking for a way
to contribute to what we felt was both morally and intellectually necessary as a two-sided history that would incorporate
narratives of the colonised along with histories of the colonisers. And there was another moral choice that I believe we
three made at this time: it was for inclusive rather than sec-
tional histories. Great redressive contributions are made by
those who, acting under similar impulses, have opted to write
histories of the oppressed; but there is the danger of a reverse
segregation in this, and we knew that we wanted to write collective histories in which the interactions of colonisers and
colonised would be studied holistically.

Now, historiography as a university discourse involves
intellectual theorising as well as moral choices. The methodology that we encouraged each other to assemble for this endeavour was mainly drawn from that branch of anthropology
that is called 'ethnography'—the study of distinct cultural practices and the worldview that informs them. We had, of course,
to adapt what we learned to our own 'field work' in the
archives, and we also joined those who were taking anthropology decisively out of its long thraldom to colonialism by
insisting that the colonisers themselves must be 'anthro-
pologised' as rigorously as any 'native'.

My first book was ethnography as I had by then come to understand it. In *The Transformation of Virginia, 1740–1790*,[1] I searched especially for reported actions, so as to reconstruct the customs and rituals that had organised a past landscape of daily life. The site of this historical-anthropological 'field work' was colonial North America—the Virginia that produced some of the first successful revolutionary leaders of the modern world, George Washington and Thomas Jefferson among them. The many-sidedness that was the intended ethic of this history was expressed in an affirmation that a people's 'landscape' is at once the most revealing and the most inclusive 'document' that can be found. In any society, everyone, male or female, humble or exalted, has their (very unequal) appropriations of space; on that they will leave 'action signatures' in which the attentive historical ethnographer can seek to 'read' their 'mark' set on life. In the same spirit, the second part of my first history went on to explore defiant new 'signatures'— the exciting invented rituals of a revolution that culminated in the 1776 casting out of the king. This was intended as a book about more than regional history; it was to be an ethnographic 'everybody's history' of what I had early learned to call 'the Atlantic democratic revolution'. My second book, just now completed, has gone deeper into the anthropological approach. *Landon Carter's Uneasy Kingdom: Revolution and Rebellion on a Virginia Plantation*[2] attends to the myths by which all action is known and directed rather than to action in itself. It is largely concerned with the cognitive turmoil accompanying the replacement of cherished old myths by new ones—a kind of 'history wars' of two hundred years ago!

The two-sided historiography that I was drawn to is precisely the account of the past that has been highlighted by the recent 'History Wars', because it has angered those who cling to an older, one-sided narrative that glorified the pioneer settlers and their self-proclaimed mission to 'civilise' those whom they dispossessed

As the battle smoke of the 'History Wars' drifts away, academic historians should ask themselves whether they might have more continuously projected their changing versions of history to a larger audience in the forms of 'public history'. As I raise that awkward question I realise that, whereas in Australia I live somewhat enclosed in the ivory tower, circumstances have given me a different involvement on the other side of the world, in the USA. I have therefore a comparative perspective to offer on questions about the relationship of academic footnoted history and patriotic-legend history in the public domain.

My ethnographic history, *The Transformation of Virginia*, has become background reading and even a kind of training manual for interpreters in one of the world's largest history museums. In consequence I have for two decades been invited to be an associate of the museum and to have some input into its program planning as well as contributing to the research base that is strenuously maintained behind the scenes. I became a participant-observer in a long-running endeavour to turn around what had, from pre- and post- World-War-II days, been an old-fashioned great-men-dominated programming that was drawn out of a matching conception of what 'patriotic' national history should be.

By the late 1970s the museum knew itself to be called upon to present history to a visiting public from a USA whose patriotic consciousness had recently been transformed by the 1960s Civil Rights movement, the concomitant Women's Liberation revolt, and the Vietnam moratorium agitation. The nation's population also was visibly changing as Latinos and Asian-Americans came into greater prominence. Williamsburg is both shrine and icon to the nation, and gets nearly a million visitors per year, so the need to develop an appropriate interpretive program is very strongly felt. In a greatly changed environment, the challenge for Colonial Williamsburg was to offer an account of the nation's past and present that was an

everybody's history, affirmative of a new commitment to inclusive democracy.

It is instructive for concerned people in Australia to consider Colonial Williamsburg's long-term project to meet its
moral obligations. The Colonial Williamsburg Foundation is
faced with a dilemma very common in the field of 'public history', where voluntary visitation not only funds the enterprise
but gives the *raison d'être*. Museums will both bankrupt themselves and defeat their own educational purposes if they make
their programs so affronting and offensive that mainstream
visitors simply stay away.

It is not surprising that the historiographic trends I have
already noted brought on 'Culture Wars' in the USA earlier
than in Australia. This is a great nation born in a revolutionary struggle for freedom and equality; it has had a recurrent
impulse to measure its history in terms of universal principles,
and to recommit itself periodically to its founding ideals. It
was no longer possible in the changed times of the 1970s and
1980s for museums to gloss over the aspects of US history that
were a bitter legacy for some and a reproach to others. Two
issues are most prominent among these troubling histories. On
the one hand, there is the recall of the violent invasions by
which Native American 'Indians' had been driven off their
ancestral lands. On the other hand, there is the enduring reproach of the long-maintained enslavement of Africans in
order to render very profitable the working of large areas of
the plundered land. (Political compromise at the time of the
Revolution had even resulted in the institution of slavery
being enshrined in the constitution of this republic founded
in the name of liberty.)

At the time of its foundation, the town of Williamsburg
had been situated far from the frontier zone of warfare with
the Indians. Therefore the aspect of America's colonising history that is shared with Australia is not appropriate for high-
lighting at that historic site. But in the age of everybody's

THE HISTORIAN'S CONSCIENCE   70

history, the museum has certainly had to deal with the fact that George Washington and Thomas Jefferson, who both first took their revolutionary stand in Williamsburg, were slave owners. Indeed half the population of that old colonial capital had been made up of men and women and children who were all enslaved.

Over some three decades now the Colonial Williamsburg Foundation has maintained and developed a Department of African American Interpretation, recruiting and deploying extremely talented guides, script writers, and historic-situation re-enactors. Every one in the foundation recognises that these programs—strong as they are—need further expansion. Nowhere near half of the costumed characters whom the visitor encounters are African Americans. But that may be impossible to achieve, since it is much easier to recruit enactors who will don hunting shirts, shoulder a musket, and follow the fife-and-drum band down the street in a march toward freedom, than it is to find descendants of slaves who—even in order to teach important history lessons—will wear the costumes and enact the demeaning roles imposed on their ancestors. And yet an impressive number of African Americans have found a vocation to develop a healing and reconciling use for a public history that teaches present-day peoples about the conditions endured by their ancestors. At the same time they engage visitors with the rich culture forged under slavery. As part of its innovative programming the foundation has systematised an account that combines history and the point-of-view of a multi-ethnic present into a challenging engagement with the long-continuing conflicts and oppressions of the past. *Becoming Americans: Our Struggle to be Free and Equal*[3] is the title of a striking illustrated volume for sale in museum shops; the same volume is the master plan for the museum's on-site historical interpretation. It identifies six contributory themes that must carry the master narrative. 'Freeing Religion' is triumphalist, since Virginia was the first modern jurisdiction to declare a total separation of church from state. Other themes challenge visitors to acknowledge a darker past. 'Possessing the Land' deals with both pioneering and the violent expulsion of the Indians. 'Enslaving Virginia' presents the cruel forms of oppression and exploitation that made the land so profitable. The culminating theme of 'Choosing Revolution' addresses the historical dilemmas faced by loyal subjects of His Britannic Majesty in 1774 when their cherished liberties were seen to be in grave danger from the Mother Country. An implied exhortation is also directed to present-day Americans: they should make a continuing commitment to the liberation work of the revolutionary generation. Is not this their legacy as citizens of a republic born of such a struggle?

But how much realism can the public stand? Film and television have gone to lengths that seem hardly applicable in face-to-face museum situations. And yet there are important lessons that cannot be taught without some shocking confrontation. Dramatisations were developed in Williamsburg that engaged audiences (always by special admission) with the traumas of sexual exploitation and of harsh physical punishment under slavery; but in 1994 there came the moment when the African American interpretation department at the Colonial Williamsburg Foundation resolved that visitors generally (and through the media, the world) should be reminded of the abuse at the heart of the institution of slavery—the trade in persons as property, regardless of their own human relationships. An actual slave auction from the colonial period would be re-enacted on the main street of the restored town: a pregnant woman would be on the block in a deceased estate sale. The owner of the father of her child would bid unsuccessfully to keep the enslaved family together by acquiring the woman. However, the operations of the market—the sale to the highest bidder—did separate the parent couple. Onlookers simultaneously knew that such denial of entitlement to family was also the fate of the unborn child.

Not surprisingly this courageous decision to associate the restored buildings of the old town with a vivid glimpse of the social system that prevailed when they were built, brought the Colonial Williamsburg Foundation right into the 'Culture Wars'. National television arranged to be there; and so did citizen action groups. At the forefront this time, however, was not the American Legion and other military veteran organisations that had acted so vociferously to block the mounting of the Smithsonian's two-sided commemoration of the nuclear-bombing of Hiroshima. Now it was veteran African American campaigners from the Civil Rights era, who would come to bear witness against this renewed demeaning of their race, as they saw it. But, with the backing of the foundation, the African Americans who had proposed the program and would be its principal re-enactors stood firm. They insisted that such an acknowledgement of the realities of a historic town with a claim to be a birth site of American liberty should be, for both blacks and whites, a positive step toward a future that would be freer of the legacies of enslavement that are still so much a part of American life. 'And those who came to mock, re-mained to pray.' Prominent protesters declared, after they had witnessed the re-enactment, that they found it a positive experience, a painful but redemptive return to a deplorable past. But, of course there also have been occasional and continuing complaints in newspapers on the right about a 'politically correct' history that teaches 'hate America'.

Another story from the implementation of Williamsburg's new master narrative may be a way to conclude these reflections. The museum interpreters found particular difficulty in facing up to their task in the year when the predominant theme for program development purposes was 'Enslaving Virginia'. Perhaps because of the anticipated resistance, the research department that supplies the basis of training produced an outsize fat folder of documents of the realities of slavery in colonial and revolutionary times, as though by weight of 'fact' to prove the point. But, in the face of awkwardness and resentment at the imposed task, probably more helpful was the suggestion that the necessarily grim story be presented in a context large enough to make its lessons acceptable. It should be yoked, as it were, to a much more recent relevant history that everybody now owns. Let it be asked: what was the most striking achievement in the public life of the United States in the twentieth century? Surely not putting men on the moon? Was it not rather the overthrow of the systematic race segregation that was still in the 1950s so prevalent in the North almost as much as the South? And because everyone knows that this work is very incomplete, museum-goers can be led to find a positive part for themselves yet to play.

What is crucial to the continuing success of Colonial Williamsburg in rendering visitors constructively thoughtful about a troubling past has been the positioning of narrators and audiences within a big story leading up to where they all now stand. The words in the title of the overall plan—'our struggle to be free and equal'—are crucial, because they imply an ongoing, forward-looking commitment. People, I believe, will 'own' the cruel parts of their history if the story that truthfully includes it invokes from participants a resolution to be part of the making of a better future.

History is better than fable only if it is founded on the complex documentary record of the past; and yet in its properly conducted forms it assuredly has an ethical function. History must, in its scholarly and its many more public tellings, suggest a story always as yet unfinished. Are we not all called upon to play positive and healing roles in its continuation? Let us remember that there are no 'facts' for the future; we have to believe that it belongs to us—to the human race—to make it more as it should be than the past has ever been.

NOTES

[1] Rhys Isaac, *The Transformation of Virginia, 1740–1790*, University of North Carolina Press, Chapel Hill, 1982.

[2] Rhys Isaac, *Landon Carter's Uneasy Kingdom: Revolution and Rebellion on a Virginia Plantation*, Oxford University Press, New York, 2004.

[3] *Becoming Americans: Our Struggle to be Free and Equal*, Colonial Williamsburg Foundation, Williamsburg, 1998.

CHAPTER 6

BEVERLEY KINGSTON

A PLEA FROM THE PERIPHERIES FOR MODESTY

Growing up as a girl in an intellectually and culturally impoverished environment made it difficult to aspire to anything, let alone writing history. It has never been possible to
make up for all those years in which there were few books and
not much stimulation. Most of the ordinary cultural heritage
of educated Australia was unknown or irrelevant in Gordonvale
and Ingham where my father worked, and Innisfail where we
spent a lot of time with my maternal grandparents in the 1940s
and 1950s. Running wild in those small north Queensland
country towns, and making up stories under the house were
no equivalent to having access to cultural resources and a
sophisticated education. I read my pocket dictionary and the
Bible from cover to cover, and knew my school readers by heart
within the first week of every year. But there were no libraries
till I was about twelve. I devoured *The Women's Weekly* until
my mother found me reading *A Town like Alice* and said it was
unsuitable for a 9-year-old. Not knowing much means you
don't respond or react to all kinds of things that are obvious to

a better informed person. Judgements are based on instinct, not knowledge or understanding. Imagination needs ideas to thrive. Knowing enough to ask useful questions or understand the implications of what you are seeing or reading is one of the constant challenges for a historian, especially a young one; the better one's knowledge, the greater the likelihood of sympathetic or imaginative engagement. I never knew enough.

Being female was much more restrictive than I realised at the time. It certainly contributed to a kind of poverty in my education, though thanks to my parents' Presbyterian background, I was never denied access to whatever formal educational opportunities were available. But they also had strong expectations that I would acquire lady-like habits of thought and behaviour. There were many things one simply did not do. It was better, my mother said, not to know about some things, easier to live in ignorance. So my curiosity was repressed and my imagination stifled by the expectation that I would become a 'lady'. Only occasionally have I been able to turn learning to be a lady to advantage or extend the insights I derived from observing and listening to my grandmother and my mother into the writing of history. To a certain extent, I suppose, my view of the world from those remote places has produced an interesting edge to the history I have written. But I have never really been able to compensate for spending so much of my life on the peripheries, both as an escapee from North Queensland, and as a failed lady in a world of men.

It is accepted wisdom today that anyone can do anything So we have banks run by managers without real knowledge of banking, retail stores managed by people who have never been behind a counter. Among historians there has been some reluctance to talk about such questions as whether men should write women's history or white people should tackle black history, whether one needs to be religious to write the history of religion and so on. I still believe that anyone can try to write any kind of history but the outcome will always be related to the quality of the input. Long ago I knew that try as

I might to enter them, in reality or in my imagination, there were many worlds that were ultimately closed to me. I know from the quality of my insight into the lives of women just how much I can't know about the lives of men. It would be extremely arrogant (and ultimately unproductive) to deny anyone the right to investigate any historical subject, but there can be no doubt that a passionate investigation by someone with inside knowledge will be very different from a coolly efficient study carried out by someone who comes initially as a complete outsider.

On another level, I also discovered that not knowing people in either Sydney or Melbourne as one knows them because you went to school or university together was a great barrier to finding out or understanding what was really going on. Perhaps if I had worked as a journalist, I might have been able to build contacts, but it is incredibly hard putting together all the little pieces of information, those scraps about ex-wives and second cousins and the family influence which explains why otherwise dull people are in positions of power from inside a university. Had I stayed in Brisbane, perhaps I would have continued to learn from contact with my university peer group, though I doubt this, because I was always shy and my northern accent (which I couldn't hear) was often deplored or ridiculed, making me both more self-conscious and defensive. Only a couple of the boys I knew from my primary schools in the north went to university, while the most interesting thing about most of the girls I knew from boarding school in Warwick was the men they married. So much history is based on shared experience, a common language and culture. Many of the debates about contemporary Australian history are about the difference between history in which it was assumed that there was a common culture (though this was not true: it was more a dominant culture) and history which has been trying to speak to the more obviously diverse culture which is now reality. I partially solved the problem of not belonging by immersing myself in the distant past where, because there were no living protagonists, there were both limits on what could ever be known or said and where the evidence had either survived or was lost forever. But I regret my inability to engage in the kind of history that is about shaping reputations and setting agendas. Though I distrust historians who assert their power to make or break public reputations, it happens, and I can understand why.

Perhaps my own experience has made me sensitive to the position of those who were powerless or had no voice in society. I certainly believe that in writing history I should try to be fair, especially to past generations who can no longer tell their own stories or protest about misrepresentation, and that I try to understand and explain them to the present. I believe also that I should try to tell any story affecting those who are still living in such a way that they recognise themselves even though they may not agree with the way I have described or accounted for their actions. Because of my own ignorance and vulnerability, I have never thought it my business to apportion praise or blame, to chastise wrongdoers or to lay down the law on anything. I am often surprised, though, at the certainty with which others, friends, colleagues, people in public life, express their views, and frequently wonder how they can be so sure or state their positions so confidently. If anything my study of history has made me less certain about everything. My mother used to complain that it stopped me from being able properly to distinguish right from wrong. I could always produce an argument for the other person's behaviour no matter how bad, she said. I must confess now, though, that the more I see of human behaviour the more sympathy I have come to feel with and for the natural world.

It must now be obvious that many earnest and sophisticated questions about the practice of history have been outside my experience. I've always felt inhibited about taking strong moral positions. I cannot recall ever having made a shocking discovery that caused me any kind of angst. Perhaps this is because I am not easily shocked and am impervious, as my mother said, to a normal sense of right and wrong. Perhaps it is simply because as an outsider, I've always been bemused by the behaviour I've observed. I may also simply have thought that whatever it was, was explicable in terms of humanities' immense capacity for cruelty, evil or wilful ignorance.

Because I know I am a product of my own limitations and they are extensive, I have never believed in the possibility of objectivity. I think that I should strive for even-handedness in my treatment or the different sides of any question, but sometimes I may not know enough to know how simple-minded or biased I am. As someone who always wanted to write and fell into history because I lacked the imagination for anything else, I have always been aware of the immense power and flexibility of language. Every time I write and re-write a sentence I marvel at the many small differences of meaning that can be achieved by slightly varying the words or their arrangement. As writing, history is capable of everything from the general impression to the precise recital of names and dates, from incisive analysis to imaginative description. In between there is scope for every style of writing from narrative to rhetoric, from poetry to jargon. And like every other writer, the historian has no control over what mental equipment or knowledge his or her readers bring to their understanding. Once the pages are published, the genie is out of the bottle, just as it is with a novel or a poem. Many of the problems of history flow from this. If the writing is too persuasive, the history can be suspect. If it is too dull or impenetrable, it is simply not read and therefore of no consequence. It is not the case that 'truth' will prevail. The truth is invariably tied up with how it is written.

But before any writing begins, there must be some research. Whether the research has been substantial or worthwhile is usually the easiest thing to discern. The historian's experience, ideas and values will inform the area of research and the approaches taken; however, everyday work practices can affect the quality of historical research. Or perhaps they are integral to ideas and the values. My own work habits pre-date photocopiers and microfilm, which means I place a great deal of importance on accuracy, effectiveness, and efficiency. I've never really adjusted to the time-consuming and space wasting practices of modern scholarship. Usually I find it just as effective to read a book in the library to get a feel of the author's tone and intention, noting places where I might need to copy a quotation or paraphrase a passage, then to go back, review, and usually cull my selections, then finally make the necessary notes. Photocopying often simply adds to the labour since there will be many pages which will have to be filed and later re-read. Deciding what is worth noting and copying it by hand requires concentration and serious engagement with the material in front of me. Only for pages of tables or statistics does wholesale photocopying seemed worthwhile.

As a student I devised for myself a method of note-taking which I later discovered was very similar to that recommended by Beatrice Webb in *My Apprenticeship*. Because I needed to maintain control over my information, each note went on to a half sheet of quarto, later A4, with a clear indication of where it came from so that I could go back to the source quickly and efficiently if necessary or quote from my notes confidently. Therefore I developed the habit of checking quotations for accuracy as I copied them. I always try to make a full bibliographical entry with accurate page numbers so that I can reliably copy the details if necessary into footnotes and bibliography. My only exception to this practice is where I am working through a long run of a newspaper or journals; then I make my notes serially on foolscap, now quarto, with a running index for date, page, column where necessary in the margin. I have found that this saves time and effort in writing a new heading for every note and provides a kind of inbuilt check on accuracy, at least as far as the dates are concerned. Needless to say, neat, clear handwriting has been a great help. The work itself often seems slow, but the care with which it has been done has probably paid off in the long run. I find too that by working so deliberately I can often write brief accounts of my reactions to the sources or analyses of their contents as I go. These are immensely valuable when I return to my notes after a long absence. But having said that, I am very aware of the likelihood that I have read selectively and not noticed things which are not part of my immediate interest. I cannot say how many times I have returned, e.g. to Anthony Trollope's account of his visit to the Australian colonies in 1871–72, and found a description of something which it seems I've never noticed before.

I expect to do all my own research which is undoubtedly why I am so slow. I've never used research assistants and I don't like to waste other people's time with vague papers or half-finished writing. I think books should be worth the cost of buying and reading them—a great many aren't. I can't stand pretension or trendiness, and I have little patience with anything not clear enough to follow at first reading. Though great complexities and much sophistication will enhance anything, if there isn't a solid foundation, it's chatter. I've no interest in argument for its own sake. Taking an opposing position may be a good way to expose weakness, but once that's done, it's done. Debates are generated and fostered to attract attention, increasingly so in our market-dominated world, but they make me impatient. Clearly, a great deal of my Presbyterian training has stuck.

When young I puzzled over the advice that I should read 'all' the 'relevant' sources if possible. This may have been feasible for a certain kind of diplomatic or administrative history, and before the advent of messy democracy, but deciding which sources were relevant and how many meant 'all' has always been a worry. I came to the conclusion that I would have to rely on 'available' rather than relevant sources, and study and use them according to my own criteria of significance. This meant that I had to justify to myself the value of each source, be able to explain what I made of it and place it in a hierarchy of significance. Therefore I needed to know as much as I could about its provenance. For example, I couldn't use a memoir written by someone who was hostile or had only paid a brief visit to make a substantial claim about some incident or person. A long run of a single source, in general, was more to be trusted because I could get a good sense of its point of view and the way it worked than many occasional sources, even though they might seem more attractive or sympathetic. The circumstances in which sources were created helped define their relevance. Highly opinionated letters by a young man to his fiancée were written for a very different purpose to those written by a branch manager to head office or by a public servant reporting to his minister. Quoting any sources verbatim usually required careful context. I long ago came to the conclusion that it was dangerous to dash at the sources, too easy to get the tone or the meaning wrong. So I hate research that has, for whatever reason, to be done on the run, and have failed to finish various projects because my research has seemed inadequate or the sources too difficult to re-visit. These days I prefer to read sources which I have identified as likely to yield good information, carefully and thoroughly, at the expense, no doubt, of lots of others which might be relevant but not necessarily more relevant. Thinking about and weighing the evidence seems just as effective as having lots of evidence which still has to be sorted, the significant from the trivial.

The fact that all history now written and researched within universities is subjected to measurement for productivity has effectively rendered irrelevant most of the ideals and practices outlined above. It has also gone a long way to destroying the quality and authority of history itself. The model on which all university research is now based, viz. investing money which will produce results which can be patented or marketed for an eventual profit, is hard to apply to history. While it is true that occasionally a volume of history becomes a bestseller, the hidden costs of producing it are enormous. How does one calculate the cost or value of keeping the records in libraries and archives or of searching out and making accessible the memories stored away in people's heads? State libraries and archives are now required to attempt to value their collections for accounting and insurance purposes, but anyone who has been involved in the process knows that the gap between the market value of a single scrap of Ned Kelly memorabilia and the value assigned to the whole of any public collection makes no arithmetical sense. Indeed if we were to give the evidence for our history its true valuation according to market principles, we couldn't afford it. And none of that takes account of the labour involved in searching, checking, evaluating and eventually, writing.

History has been badly served by the modern drive too, to specialisation and professionalisation. Though we have been trying to pretend it is otherwise, no qualifications are actually necessary, no training is really required to research or write history. There is nothing very special about history or mysterious about how it is done. Certainly, some training can make research more efficient and effective, but the crucial thing is the desire to know as much as can be known about some aspect of the past. Some of our best history has been written by journalists or by passionate enthusiasts. The idea of history as a profession with a set of skills to be taught and examined cannot be sustained. Bad history is not life threatening like a faulty bridge or a wrongly diagnosed illness. At worst we can deceive ourselves, defame the dead, or infuriate the living. Though modesty is also a crime in today's self-promoting and inflated culture, historians have no choice but to be modest about what they can do and hope to be thought useful. So perhaps it is a good thing that I have always been peripheral. With too many people like me, there'd not be much history at all.

CHAPTER 7

JOHN HIRST

CHANGING MY MIND

Historians write from the evidence, but also from their understanding of how the world works and how they would like it to work. A historian who thinks large impersonal forces have shaped our destiny will write a different history from one who thinks that great leaders have turned the tide—or made a tide. A socialist will not write approvingly of the rise of modern capitalist society. A free marketeer will be hard put to treat socialists sympathetically.

The great majority of the historians of Australia over the last forty or fifty years have been left-leaning, progressive people. I was taught Australian history by them and their books. I was brought up on Russel Ward *The Australian Legend* (1958) and Robin Gollan *Radical and Working Class Politics* (1960); my first teacher at the University of Adelaide in the early 1960s was Ian Turner. These three, as it happens, were more than left-leaning: they had all been members of the Communist Party. They were all properly trained academic historians and none was a crude propagandist. They wrote under tighter control of their discipline than the next generation of radicals. I still value and draw on their books. But their sympathies were plain.

My sense of how the world works and my political allegiance were at first those of my teachers. They are now different. With this change, my history-writing has changed. I am not sure how these two changes relate to each other. I wonder if my study of history has changed my views or whether my views changed and then my history-writing.

By the time I acquired my BA I believed that the Labor Party was the only party decent people could support. Labor promised a new, just social order; Liberals were the tools of big business, selfish and stupid.

I proceeded immediately to study for a PhD. The topic I chose for my thesis required me to study the South Australian history of both the Labor and Liberal parties. They both had their origins in Adelaide; the Labor party in the trade unions and the Liberals among the city's businessmen and large property holders. If either group was to be a governing party, it had to gain support in the country. It took them some time to realise that country people were not automatically going to support a city organisation and its program.

The Labor Party had to drop its plan to tax all land, big farms and small, and it had to give country branches a real say at conferences. With these concessions made, it did win office in its own right for the first time in 1910. But the hard men in the trade unions were disgusted at the moderation of the Labor government. It had not immediately implemented the whole Labor platform! They turned on the Labor politicians, one of whose offences was to have made these concessions to the country. During World War I the hard men expelled the leading Labor politicians (for supporting conscription) and they reduced country branches to a nullity at Labor conferences. In future delegates had as many votes as the number of members they represented. A trade union delegate might have 10 000 votes and a country branch delegate 10.

As I followed this struggle, I found my sympathies were very much with parliamentarians. I was a Labor supporter (I was never a party member) but I was perfectly happy for parliamentarians to accept the restraints that winning government required.

The Liberal Party in South Australia took final shape in 1910, the year Labor first ruled. Most of its money came from big business and large landholders, but they had no influence over the choice of candidates. In the countryside, which was the Liberals' stronghold, party-members insisted on selecting their own candidates without interference from head office. The farmers who wanted more land for themselves and their sons had also insisted that the party program include the compulsory purchase by the government of large pastoral estates and their subdivision into farms. It was to resist just such a measure that the big businessmen and landowners had first formed a political organisation. Now they were bankrolling a party that supported it! They were not happy.

The discipline of studying the evidence had led me to put aside the view that Liberals were just the voice of big business. But I was unusual among Australian historians in spending time on the Liberal Party. When they write political history, they generally study causes with which they sympathise. Some years ago an American colleague of mine expressed his amazement at this narrowness: 'There are shelves of books in the library on the Labor Party, even a small shelf on Communists and the Communist Party, but you are lucky to find two or three volumes on the Liberal Party—but haven't they governed the country for most of its history?' The imbalance is not quite as bad as this. Part of the difference arises because Liberals themselves are not as interested in their history and write fewer memoirs and reminiscences. But I think academic historians can be criticised for their lack of interest in the Liberals or for simply adopting the Labor view of them. You might think that left-leaning historians would study them if only to understand the enemy. Fortunately we now have two very revealing books on the Liberals written by left-leaning Judith Brett: *Robert Menzies' Forgotten People* and *The Australian Liberals and the Moral Middle Class*.

So why was I more ready to spend time on the Liberals? Was it just that I was writing a general history and I needed to look at them as well as Labor? Or was it that my mother was a Liberal voter and did not appear to be the willing tool of big business? She voted Labor for the first time in 1966 (against the land-slide for Harold Holt) because she did not want my younger brother to be conscripted for Vietnam. She was not a passionate or a vocal Liberal; she did not take much interest in politics. She was calm and non-judgemental; very unwilling to see wickedness. This is a useful trait for a historian who first of all has to understand.

If I was now less prejudiced about the Liberal Party, my political sympathies still lay with Labor and they strengthened when Gough Whitlam became leader. I was as elated by his 1972 victory and as angry at his 1975 dismissal as any party member.

My bedrock assumptions about the world changed while I was writing my book on convict society in New South Wales. It was published in 1983 when I was forty years old. I began my researches with the usual assumption that convict society was cruel and degraded with masters being corrupted by the power they held over the convicts. The question I posed for myself was how had this brutalised society been transformed into a free, democratic society. My conclusion was that I had asked the wrong question. This was not a brutalised society; it was much more a normal British colony which had convicts as part of its labour force and which had always preserved crucial legal rights and economic opportunities for convicts

and ex-convicts. I was one of what is now called 'the normalising school' on convict society.

At the centre of the book were musings on the nature of
power. As my ideas formed, I found I was contesting the liberal view that power corrupts and that if subordinates complain
or rebel it is because they have been badly treated. I began the
section in the book on masters and servants by questioning how
much power the masters of convict servants had. They had the
power to get their convicts flogged, but they got poorer service
than the masters back in England with servants who were kept
in line by the threat of being sacked without a reference. Even
under threat of flogging, convict servants were inclined to be
stroppy, to get drunk or run away. A minority were absolutely
incorrigible. I explored the idea that some masters were driven
to cruelty not by lust for power but through the frustrations of
getting work out of convicts, of not having enough power.
Cruelty was a standing temptation for those who began by
thinking that gentle treatment would bring good service. The
commonly accepted formula for success with convicts was a
combination of kindness and firmness (that could include
flogging). This was the practice of those known—by convicts
and others—as 'good masters', an old notion of power being
exercised justly that survived even in the convict colony.

I was more open to think in new ways about convict society because I had read the recent books on slavery in the
United States which described a complex relationship between
masters and slaves. In law slaves might be property to be
bought and sold but slaves were not things, for things do not
answer back, go slow or run away. I had also learnt the para-
dox that when you 'own' your labour force you are more
responsible for its welfare than when you hire free workers for
wages. More important, I think, was the fact that I was now a
'master' myself—of a very rebellious teenager. I was of course
a decent and understanding parent but that did not lessen the
ferociousness of the rebellion. I was under siege myself as I
watched masters trying to control convicts. My fellow-spirit

in convict Sydney was the very decent Christian master George Allen. He was reluctant to send his servants to court for punishment, but when John Crawley ignored his orders on the pretence that he was deaf, he felt he had no option. On the day Crawley returned after receiving twenty-five lashes, Allen noted in his diary: 'It is very strange that when Men are well treated they will not behave themselves'.

My family, without having read my convict book, but having some sense of its argument, mocked me for claiming that flogging did not hurt. Some of my colleagues made the same criticism in a different way. But in fact I pointed out that flogging did injure some convicts so badly that they were admitted to hospital. It was not true, as is sometimes alleged, that flogging was used as a punishment because it did not take the convict away from his work. What I did not do in my book was to denounce flogging and be constantly outraged by it. By our standards it is an outrage, but I have this historian's quirk of knowing that the people who flogged criminals would think our practice of locking criminals up in all male institutions for thirty years or more cruel and unnatural. So I hesitate to condemn the past, but I recognise that I run the danger of not seeing horror when it is truly there.

The writing of my convict book set my mind in a new direction. Like a good historian I can offer the evidence for this in the notable sayings I have recorded in a little notebook I always have with me.

> History shows there is no such thing as absolute power
> (F. Eggleston, *State Socialism in Victoria*, p. 315)

> Mild, just, but exact in discipline; he was father to his people who were attached to him from affection and obedient from confidence
> (Tribute to James Cook on contemporary monument, copy in Maritime Museum Greenwich)

> Surely of all the 'rights of man', this right of the ignorant man to
> be guided by the wiser, to be gently or forcibly held in the true
> course by him is the indisputablest
>
> (Thomas Carlyle, *Chartism*, chapter 6)

Thomas Carlyle, the historian-philosopher of the nineteenth
century, became my favourite guide. He lived through the
industrial revolution and hated its tendency to reduce all
human relations to a cash nexus. But he did not believe that
the liberal and democratic programs of his day would meet
humankind's deepest needs. I was myself living in a new age of
revolution, the libertarianism of the 1970s and after. I could
not believe its promise that the loosening of social ties and the
questioning of all authority would produce a better world. It
was on this issue that I parted company with left-leaning, progressive people. I was, and am still, a supporter of the old left
causes of a fairer distribution of wealth and opportunity.

I do not have the temperament of the liberationist. When
authority is attacked my instinct is to come to its defence. I am
very sympathetic to the problems of governing. I think our
society has become too suspicious of authority and forgetful
that we have cultural restraints on power that have produced
and may still produce good leaders, bosses and teachers. The
modern formula for governing is to be open and accountable
and to consult widely and be inclusive. But the pleasures of
sitting in committees can be exaggerated. In a committee we
are instantly aware that some people are more fluent, forth-
right and determined than others; that we are not equals. With
a good boss we are all equals in that he or she is equally concerned for us and will judge us equitably. That is a very satisfy-
ing environment in which to work.

I was not favouring a more authoritarian government for
the state. There we need the checks and balances. The danger,
as I saw it, was that democratic principles and rights were
being applied to all subordinate institutions, which rendered
them less able to do their job. A school that has so little

control over its pupils that it has to call in the police is a failed institution.

From Carlyle, who was much influenced by German idealist philosophy, I received the encouragement to think differently about human motivation and the course of history. Here are some extracts from my notebook.

> It is a calumny on men to say that they are roused to heroic action by ease, hope of pleasure, recompense—sugar plums of any kind, in this world or the next. In the meanest mortal there lies something nobler. The poor swearing soldier, hired to be shot, has his 'honour of the soldier', different from drill regulations and the shilling a day. It is not to taste sweet things, but to do noble and true things, and vindicate himself under God's heaven as a god-made Man that the poorest son of Adam dimly longs . . . Difficulty, abnegation, martyrdom, death are the *allurements* that act on the heart of man.
>
> (Carlyle, *On Heroes and Hero-worship*, Lecture 2)

> It is not what a man outwardly has or wants that constitutes the happiness or misery of him . . . The real smart is the soul's pain and stigma, the hurt inflicted in the moral self.
>
> (Carlyle, *Chartism*, chapter 5)

From my teachers in Australian history I learned a sort of debased Marxism which looked to economic interests to explain events. This was somewhat offset by the lectures Professor Hugh Stretton gave on European history. I was probably not well attuned to his message. I do remember gaining a sense that the world was more open than is sometimes portrayed and that men with fresh ideas can be influential. In an aside he declared that the trouble with the Labor Party was that it had stopped thinking, which was no doubt true of the Labor Party circa 1963, pre Whitlam. We students were in the dark about Stretton. He had written nothing, though he was rumoured to be working on a magnum opus of whose subject there were conflicting reports. It was only later that all became clear when I read *The Political Sciences* and *Ideas for Australian Cities*.

The Australian historians had done a regular job on the history of the making of the Australian Commonwealth. I can remember at university reading on the economic interests that underlay the federation movement. Many times thereafter I had to read that federation was a business deal with very little idealism about it. It gave me great satisfaction for the celebration of the hundredth anniversary of Federation in 2001 to write a book that inverted this claim, and put the ideal before the material.

My book began with the idealists, the people who worked for federation who called it, publicly and privately, a noble, holy or sacred cause. That was the first sign that the old interpretation had missed the animating spirit of the movement. My job then was to explain why the making of a nation could be viewed this way. I hope I was not too starry eyed about these people. They had an interest in the creating of a nation, not an economic interest but a status interest, the quintessential selfish interest, what Carlyle called the moral self. They wanted to avoid the stigma of being thought second-rate. While the colonies were separate those who lived in them were known as colonists, a second-class people. If the colonies combined, the colonists would become citizens of a nation and share the standing of other nations round the globe.

Businessmen wanted the colonies to combine. My knock-down case against their influence on federation was that they wanted a customs union, not a federation. A customs union would yield immediate economic benefits: this was the practical proposal. Federation would deliver a customs union but since it involved the setting up of a whole new system of government it would be immensely difficult and would take too long. Until the very last, businessmen opposed moves to federation.

Over many years the businessmen advanced plans for a customs union, but they always failed because of the different economic interests and policies of the different colonies. It was the 'impractical' men, the politicians, the patriots and the poets, who created the union, which then delivered a customs union.

I called my book *The Sentimental Nation*. I think of it as a tribute to Carlyle. It has of course to pass the test of the discipline: has the evidence been produced to support this interpretation? But the making of an interpretation of this sort is also evidence of what has happened to my mind and self since I left my first teachers.

CHAPTER 8

MARILYN LAKE

ON HISTORY AND POLITICS

When I was young, my history was fiery with the political exuberance of youth. I denounced the capitalists and cheered on the workers, praised the republicans (when I could find any) and mocked the lickspittle imperialists. In writing about the political divisions on the home front during World War I for my MA thesis, I was fervent in my identifications and sympathies, ridiculing the pro-war jingoes and idealising the brave anti-conscriptionists and pacifists, who dared to take them on. My hero was Clifford Hall, an anti-war activist who enlisted with the field ambulance and was killed on the Western Front in 1915.

Though I scorned and excoriated the Win-the-War parties —and concluded my first book, *A Divided Society*, based on the thesis, with a chapter called 'Triumph—for hatreds old and new', I think in retrospect I did little to explain the wartime political triumph of conservatism.[1] The times in which I wrote were not conducive to such endeavour—it was the early 1970s and as I researched the thesis, Labor won government federally for the first time in twenty-three years, the first election in which I cast a vote. I was more interested in celebrating the defeat of political conservatism than understanding its earlier successes.

Fortunately, though, I was offered some timely advice about the writing of history. A kind reviewer commended the liveliness and passion of my study, but suggested that I should do more to *explain* the ascendancy of conservative, imperialist and xenophobic groups, rather than simply take aim at them. Why did Australians respond to the imperial embrace and forego the independence espoused earlier by leaders such as Higgins and Deakin? Why did we cease to be a social laboratory? Why did Australia become so isolationist? I have recently returned to these questions with renewed interest.

And I have since come to believe that our distinctive ethical obligation as historians is *explanation*: to explain the past—people's choices and their sense of themselves—to people living in the present. This interpretative act entails a double set of duties: to those in the past, whom we presume in our conceit to represent, including those with whom we might most strongly disagree; and to our readers and interlocutors in the present, whom we must convince through the collection of evidence, the telling of a good story and the construction of persuasive argument. Sometimes the balancing of these duties —reconciling one's obligations to the past and the present— can be a fraught undertaking.

As their self-appointed interpreters, we must try to understand what our historical subjects were about, to grasp their intended meanings and unintended effects, to comprehend their contexts and subjectivities, to enter their world. But we need to write about our subjects in this world. We must communicate our findings in terms that are comprehensible, and perhaps acceptable, to our contemporaries. Paradoxically, historians are required to make sense of the difference and strangeness of people in the past through a process of identification. Humanist empathy underpins most good historical writing. Arguably, it was in his lack of imaginative empathy for

Aboriginal Tasmanians as fellow human beings and historical agents that Keith Windschuttle, in *The Fabrication of Aboriginal History*, failed most signally as a historian. But Windschuttle was putting history at the service of a political project: he was writing in defence of his nation and to attack those whom he believed were its traducers.[2]

As politically minded citizens living in the present, we might often be tempted to construct a past that best suits current political needs. Or we set up a court of judgement, calling the past to account for its failings and commending those who, 'before their time', advanced more enlightened or progressive views. We might be tempted to write history as a record of heroes and villains, winners and losers, oppressors and victims. In our time, the urge to pass judgement on the past and to substitute accusation ('racist', 'reactionary', 'criminal', 'primitive', 'puritan') for analysis seems particularly strong, but good history and good politics are not the same project, and indeed may often be at odds, the complexity of historical analysis undermining, or inhibiting, the simplifying binary logic of effective politics. History should generate complex understanding; politics thrives on dichotomies and demands that one choose between sides.

The tension between our commitments as engaged citizens and our professional obligations as historians becomes most pronounced when our subjects held views now considered oppressive and long since discredited. For the most persuasive explanations can easily be read as *apologia*—or advocacy. Such, I think, is the historian's occupational hazard. But the common and condescending defence that the benighted ones were simply 'people of their time' is just as inadequate, in historical and intellectual terms, as is the umbrella charge of 'racism'. Neither formulation promotes historical understanding.

I want to explore these issues at greater length with reference
to two areas of my own research: maternalist feminism between
the 1890s and 1930s; and the race thinking of national leaders,
such as Alfred Deakin and H. B. Higgins. Maternalist feminists
were also race thinkers, who nevertheless attempted to forge
alliances across racial divisions—invoking the common ground
of motherhood—with Aboriginal women, especially in South
Australia and Western Australia. To attempt to represent these
feminists' ideas and political strategies has, however, been a
challenging task—with readers ready to reprimand my, and
my subjects', perceived ideological failings, and in particular
my apparent blindness to my subjects' conservatism, paternalism, heterosexism and racism.

Whereas I had assumed that my ethical obligation as a historian was to make sense of—to make meaningful—the historical specificity of my subjects' views, some critics (especially
non-historians) wanted to charge me with complicity with
a seemingly monolithic and entirely regrettable thing called
'middle-class white feminism'.[3] I had in fact already published
analytical essays exploring the colonial 'whiteness' of Australian
feminists in a British journal, back in 1993 and 1994.[4]

My decision to write a history of feminism in Australia
was inspired, of course, by my own identification with feminist
politics, but also, importantly, by my more general interest in
the history of political ideas, such as citizenship, independence, nationalism and race and the impact of sexual difference
on their formulation. In most histories of Australian politics,
feminists were not considered to be doing politics: and they
could not, apparently, be conceptualised as engaged in 'political struggle'.[5]

But in my proposed history of feminism, who should
count as feminist? Certainly not all women or even all women
activists. Too often the categories 'feminist' and 'woman' were
conflated, especially by those who had no interest in either.
But as I emphasised in the introduction to *Getting Equal: The*

History of Australian Feminism, 'feminism is a politics, not an effect of biology'.[6] (It was the publisher, by the way, who insisted on the definitive article in my title, signalling a presumption of authority on my part that would provoke much feminist wrath: did I have an ethical obligation, or the power, to resist this publishing ploy?)

Who would count as feminist in my history? Over the years, feminists have appeared in many guises. The feminist of one era can look like an oppressor in another: in one age sexual freedom might be regarded as the source of women's oppression, while in another it's integral to women's liberation; one hundred years ago temperance was central to the feminist vision; forty years ago feminists fought for the right to drink in public bars. Definitions of feminism have changed radically over time, but contemporary feminists often imply that feminists in the past did not measure up to our exacting contemporary political standards. Indeed, earlier feminist preoccupation with what we might now call 'family values' seemed to raise questions about their eligibility to be counted as feminist at all—even though they embraced the label for themselves, while at the same time labour women (with whom we can now more readily identify) were warned off such identifications by labour men, who muttered darkly about 'sex antagonism' and 'class disloyalty'.

Nowadays, we think of feminists as those who opposed traditional sex roles, believed in equality with men and who supported women taking up paid work and political careers. Yet contemporary yardsticks might not provide a reliable guide to the radicalism of past politics. I was acutely aware of the difficulties in making comprehensible feminist views long since discredited or repudiated by those who learnt about the iniquity of sex roles in the 1970s and homophobia in the 1980s and racism in the 1990s, and thus were more 'advanced' in their thinking than all who came before them.

Yet it still seemed to me that one of the most powerful and long-lived phases of feminism in Australia was that now dubbed maternal feminism. Its spokeswomen included a diverse bunch: Rose Scott, Vida Goldstein, Ada Bromham, Alice Henry, Edith Cowan, Bessie Rischbieth, Edith Waterworth and Jessie Street, women who dominated feminist thinking and activism between the 1890s and 1940s. They were especially influential in Australia for three reasons: they had acquired full political rights at the national level in 1902, they led the new organisations that flourished post-suffrage and their ascendancy co-incided with the inauguration of the new Commonwealth of Australia, whose policy they were determined to shape. They led the world in experimenting with the potential of women's citizenship.

But much of their thinking is alien. They were maternal-ists. They believed that women's work as carers equipped them with a distinctive perspective and set of values which they would bring to bear in shaping public policy, and also that women were especially well fitted to fill new administrative and supervisory positions in the state. Thus Vida Goldstein in a pamphlet 'Why Women Should Use the Vote' urged: 'Wherever women and children are in subjection, supervision by women is necessary and women should secure the appoint-ment of women as inspectors of asylums, boarded out chil-dren, hospitals, schools and gaols'.[7] Feminists were successful in this ambition: women were appointed to a range of such positions during these decades.

It seemed to me that my task as historian was to analyse and explain this distinctive and gendered understanding of citizen-ship, to assess the extent of feminists' achievement and the limits of their thinking and to explain why their apparently conservative views were regarded in their time as revolution-ary and deeply threatening. I wrote several analytical articles on the subject—published overseas as well as in Australia—as well as sections in a number of books.[8] But, the more detailed my explanations and the more enthusiastic my analyses of these feminists' thinking as I traced the impact of sexual difference on conceptions of citizenship, the more I came to be identified with their politics. This was an unexpected and unfortunate fate for an ardent Women's Liberationist—even one who had since had two children.

It is true that in getting to know some of these feminists through my extensive researches, I came to admire them for their courage, energy, eloquence and resilience. I also noted their authoritarianism, imperiousness and jealous rivalries—characteristics not confined to feminists between the wars. They were strong individuals who took pleasure in their politics: modern Ada Bromham driving her car across the Nullarbor in 1916; Bessie Rischbieth in spine-tingling ecstasy as she listened to Charlotte Perkins Gilman in London; Jessie Street lecturing the men of the labour movement about women's right to an individual wage; the women of the United Associations singing 'Wild, Wild, Women' in their rooms in Market Street, Sydney.

Providing a sense of these human stories was central to the account I wanted to tell of the history of feminist activism—and an essential aspect of my obligations both to my subjects and my readers. Many reviewers commended the lively narrative; others denounced the roll-call of white middle-class women. My stern critics overlooked my analysis of the limited thinking of my subjects, the ways in which maternalists locked women into an identity as mothers which would rebound on them and constructed women as sexualised victims in need of feminist protection, preferring to cast me as the maternalist champion. In doing my empathetic duty by my historical subjects, I had earned the censure of contemporary feminist critics. And who needed to know about maternal feminism when the conservative backlash was in full swing, child care centres were being closed, and we were confronting the End of Equality?

Historians like to tell good stories, but in explaining the past to the present, the role of critical analysis is also crucial. Yet analysis implies, and maybe requires, detachment, which might seem problematic when one's subject is racism. Should we not simply denounce its exponents and document its destructive effects? Should I have denounced my feminist subjects who aspired to protect Aboriginal women for their 'paternalism'? When we document the efforts of those who worked against racism—such as Ada Bromham and Mary Montgomerie Bennett—do we seek really to defend or excuse their larger racist assumptions? When we seek to explain racism do we thereby justify it? Is 'guilt' a useful category when analysing the past?

My current project seeks to explore the thinking and intellectual formation of those national leaders of the early twentieth century who identified with the subject position 'the white man' and strove in his name to build 'white men's countries'. It seems to me essential to understand the centrality of race thinking to our national formation in order to free ourselves from its powerful and repressive legacies. It is also essential to understanding our relations to other peoples and places in the world—and to understanding Australia's decision to join in coalition with two other white men's countries in waging war in Iraq.

At the end of the nineteenth and into the twentieth centuries, a number of demographically diverse countries—South Africa, the United States, Kenya, Canada, New Zealand, Australia—defined themselves as 'white men's countries' in response to the threats posed by unprecedented movements of population, especially the great migrations of the British, Chinese and Indians and the beginnings of political mobilisations in support of racial equality and colonial liberation. Australia's notorious 'dictation test' was not the first of its kind. The device of introducing 'education' tests to implement racial discrimination in franchise or immigration law was first introduced in Mississippi in 1890, then Natal, then British Columbia, then Australia.

Understanding the power and permutations of race thinking in the late nineteenth century and early twentieth centuries

—at the time when the new Commonwealth of Australia was inaugurated in an act of racial expulsion with the passage of the Pacific Islands Labourers Act—it is necessary to explore the intellectual and political formation of a group of key political leaders such as A. Inglis Clark, Alfred Deakin, H. B. Higgins, W. M. Hughes and Chris Watson, in their transnational context. A global analytic frame enables us to see the relationship between Australian developments and events and thinking in Africa, the Americas and Asia. We have an obligation to identify the transnational contexts—historical, intellectual and political—in which the utopian experiment of White Australia unfolded.

To explain the project of White Australia we need to investigate and explain the gendered and racialised subjectivities of the men—the anxious men—who were its authors. Too often the history of racial ideas in Australia has been written as if they were free-floating abstractions with a dynamism all their own—or the expressions of political interests, of capital or labour, for example. But such explanations ignore the connection between the personal and the political in history, and their gendering, to which Deakin himself drew attention in 1901. Deakin and his fellow politicians spoke of their anxieties in relation to nation and race: the legislation was so important, he said, because it spoke to the instinct of self-preservation 'for it is nothing less than the national manhood, the national character and the national future that are at stake'.[9] Why was their manhood at stake? The British could never understand, said another, how important race was to Australian manhood. But why was race so important to manhood? This is what we need to explain.

The context of British imperial relations is clearly all important here—with the Colonial Office insisting on the equality of status of all colonial British subjects, whether Indian, Chinese, African or Australian, all the while refusing most British subjects the right of self-government. In response to the Colonial Office, the Australian colonials argued for the significance of another dichotomy, that between ruling and non-ruling races, those fit to govern themselves and others, and those deemed incapable of doing so. Hence the importance of Australian colonial claims to govern British New Guinea, which were also negotiated with the British during 1901, the same year as the Immigration Restriction Act and the Pacific Islands Labourers Act were passed. Australians knew they were on trial in British New Guinea (renamed Papua from 1906)—their capacity to administer the natives always open to question.

The architects of White Australia considered that they were at the cutting edge of world historic developments—and their experiment was often received as such, both by admirers and critics. Is it possible any longer to communicate the excitement of their adventure? Central to the vision was H. B. Higgins' idea that the Commonwealth of Australia was creating a new 'civilisation' that enshrined the status and self-respect of the white working man through the institution of the Commonwealth Court of Conciliation and Arbitration and its establishment of the family wage through the Harvester judgement. To explain this inter-twining of class egalitarianism and racist exclusion—the interdependence of what we might regard as progressive and reactionary politics—has been one of the most difficult, but unavoidable tasks of Australian historians. Is it possible, or acceptable to put the case without sounding defensive?

The ethics of historians are the ethics of humanists. But we have obligations to our past subjects and present day readers that may not be reconcilable—and in any case readers themselves comprise a diverse constituency, having mixed and invariably conflicting interests. Diverse audiences demand a diversity of histories and we surely have a collective obligation to encourage such proliferation.

Historians' ethical obligations arise from their commitment as humanists, but history's past exclusions—the discipline's relentless focus on the experience of white men only—reveal how narrow has been the conception of 'human' operating at the heart of history. This has been one of feminism's fundamental objections to traditional conceptions of, and scholarship in, the Humanities. I think we should encourage historians' humanist commitments, but also demand that the definition of human be always expanded to encompass the historical agency—and moral status—of those many groups who are sometimes assumed to have no history worth mentioning, such as the Tasmanian Aborigines.

Why work on white men then? Why spend time investigating the architects of White Australia? Why seek to place them in context, to empathise? One answer is because in their anxiety and defensiveness, their ambition and idealism, their poignancy and power, they were human too.

NOTES

[1] Marilyn Lake, *A Divided Society: Tasmania During World War I*, Melbourne University Press, Melbourne, 1975.

[2] For a more extended discussion of this point see Marilyn Lake, 'History and the nation' in Robert Manne (ed.), *Whitewash*, Black Inc., Melbourne, 2003.

[3] See, for example, Jenna Mead, 'Feminist history', *Australian Book Review*, 217, December 1999/January 2000, pp. 14–15.

[4] Marilyn Lake, 'Colonised and colonising: The white Australian feminist subject', *Women's History Review*, 2(3), 1993, pp. 377–86; Marilyn Lake, 'Between old world "barbarism" and "stone age primitivism": The double difference of the white Australian feminist subject', in Norma Grieve and Ailsa Burns (eds), *Australian women: Contemporary Feminist Thought*, Oxford University Press, Melbourne, 1994, pp. 80–91.

[5] For a recent and egregious example, see Robert Manne (ed.), *The Australian Century Political Struggle in the Building of a Nation*, Text Publishing, Melbourne, 1999.

6   Marilyn Lake, *Getting Equal: The History of Australian Feminism*, Allen & Unwin, Sydney, 1999, p. 16.

7   Lake, *Getting Equal*, pp. 58–9.

8   See, for example, Marilyn Lake, ' "A revolution in the family": The challenge and contradiction of maternal citizenship', in Seth Koven and Sonya Michel (eds), *Mothers of a New World: Maternalist Politics and Welfare States in Comparative Perspective*, Routledge, New York, 1993, pp. 378–95; Marilyn Lake, 'The inviolable woman: Feminist conceptions of citizenship in Australia 1900–1945', *Gender and History* (UK), 8(2), August 1996, reprinted in Joan Landes (ed.), *Feminism: The Public and the Private Oxford Readings in Feminism*, Oxford University Press, Oxford, 1998, pp. 228–47; Marilyn Lake and Katie Holmes (eds), *Freedom Bound II: Documents on Women in Modern Australia*, Allen & Unwin, 1995, Part 1; Patricia Grimshaw, Marilyn Lake, Ann McGrath and Marian Quartly, *Creating a Nation*, McPhee Gribble/Penguin, 1994.

9   Quoted in Marilyn Lake, 'On being a white man, Australia circa 1900', in Hsu Ming Teo and Richard White (eds), *Cultural History in Australia*, Allen & Unwin, Sydney, 2003, p. 100.

CHAPTER 9

PENNY RUSSELL

ALMOST BELIEVING: THE ETHICS OF HISTORICAL IMAGINATION

Most of us think we know the difference between fact and fiction. In daily life we draw unthinking distinctions between the observable phenomena of the material world and the phantasms of imagination; between responsible accounts of actual social events and invented stories which—however they may beguile or disturb—possess the ultimate comforting assurance that they didn't *really* happen. Our reactions, decisions, sheer physical movement through the world, are directed by commonsense assumptions of what is, and what is not, real.

Academic disciplines fall loosely into those that deal with the real—science, medicine, engineering—and those that deal with the creative imagination—literature, art, music, performance. The social sciences, less readily categorisable, belong with the real insofar as they employ objective, verifiable methods of research and testing, and concern themselves with the tangible, experiential realities of the social world.

And then there is history. History stands at a point of transition, impelled equally towards both realms. Reaching towards social science, historical research proceeds by collation, synthesis, scrutiny, analysis. It demands attention to detail, rigorous respect for evidence, awareness of contradictions, assessments of validity, careful paper trails of documentation. The cardinal sins of history are the omission, falsification or misrepresentation of sources. There are no excuses for telling the past as it wasn't, for lying about one's findings, for making things up.

And yet, history depends upon imagination. The past is always with us, but only inside our heads—none the less powerful for that, but curiously resistant to verification and cross-checking. When the sources are ambiguous, contradictory or simply absent, we cannot take a quick trip to the thirteenth century to see how things really were, who said what, what was happening outside the window at the time. Instead we build from inadequate, frustrating, patchily illuminating records a version of the past that satisfies our sense of what is—or was—possible; that matches the records yet remains the product of present imagination, present concerns, and the limits of present knowledge.

Historians write with intent to build their version of the past in the imagination of their readers. Good history, as Keith Hancock said, demands attachment, and attachment demands the engagement of the imagination through story. Writing history, therefore, is a creative art. It requires empathy, intuition, a keen sense of drama and pathos, a distinct narrative flair. That is why the best history is also literature; why, perhaps, works of history are more likely than works of sociology to win literary awards.

These twin imperatives—the verification of the real, and the engagement of the imagination—spawn a great diversity of practice. In the scholarly journals of academic history, or in research theses, you often find pages where the space occupied by the article itself is exceeded by a mass of footnotes in tiny font, explicating the origin of each thought, acknowledging intellectual debt and listing numerous examples from the archives which would further support the case, if only there were room to discuss them. In the slimmed-down volumes that most publishers send forth, many of those references dis-appear; pages of qualification, evidence and argumentation are ditched; and the book—if it is a good one—presents a stirring distillation of stories and their significance. Some historians therefore eschew book publishing as a 'dumbing down' of their scholarship: others embrace it, believing that scholarship only begins to count at the point when it is read.

There are also, of course, fashions within history—periods when the possibilities of quantitative method are all the rage, when faith in the real gives way to theoretical abstractions about the nature of knowledge itself, when history is accepted as a literary, interpretive medium, or when curiously misunder-stood laws of objectivity lead to the denunciation of inter-pretive work as 'fabrication'. Through such evolutions an idea of truthfulness bends, morphs and continually re-emerges. Thomas Carlyle scorned the 'Dryasdust' scholars who patiently patched together the documents of the past. He wrote instead with an impassioned creativity, seeking to distil a higher Truth of humanity and history, a Truth that could be found not in dusty parchment but only with a 'seeing heart'.[1] His younger German contemporary Leopold von Ranke by contrast 'codified the disciplinary procedures of archivally based scholar-ship', and insisted that the past did not yield 'timeless truths': each epoch must be understood in its own terms.[2] In our own day, Inga Clendinnen passionately invokes the responsibilities of the historian who bears witness to past reality, and Tom Griffiths evokes the attractions of history, where 'imagination must work in creative friction with a given world . . . a world out there that humbles and disciplines'.[3] Whether Truth is seen to reside in the archives themselves, in the shadowy world that produced them, in the heart of the writer or the integrity of the interpretation, it constrains, directs and inspires historical writing. However creative, literary, imaginative, moral and politicised history may be, it establishes a relationship of trust and responsibility between writer and reader. In that implied contract, history is not fiction: historians make stories, but they do not make them up.

How is a relationship of trust established? How do historians demonstrate honesty of purpose and practice, persuade us that they are not presenting fictions in authoritative guise? Keith Windschuttle would like us to believe that trust relies on proof, and that the proof of honest, truthful practice lies in the footnotes. And of course that is the first, self-evident role of footnotes. A footnote says, 'I did not make up the passage I have just quoted, or the event I have just described. I found it right *there*, in that precise spot, and you, too, will find it if you look.' Sometimes, however, the footnote's claim can seem to go further, to assert that in that place lies evidence of a fixed meaning which supports the present interpretation. Treated as assertions of proof, footnotes seem designed to lend authority to the text, to pin the uncertainties of the unknowable past to the reassuring but illusory solidity of 'hard evidence'. They fling a barrier between the scepticism of the reader and the vulnerability of historical knowledge. They look like a vaunting display of scholarship, academic status and authority.

But they can bear a very different message. Footnotes can refer readers back to the primary sources, not as proof or 'self-justificatory' baggage, but with a humility that acknowledges 'other possible worlds, other possible visions', empowering readers to make different conclusions, rendering the historian vulnerable to continued reinterpretation.[4] Footnotes lay careful trails of uncertainty through the apparent certainties of analysis. They inspire most trust when they signal the historian's refusal of ultimate authority.

If trust depended on the proof of footnotes, a historian who failed to meet the implied contract, who misdirected readers to a source which did not in fact contain the quoted information, failed to direct them at all, or—cardinal sin—simply made the reference up, would dissipate trust in a flash. And yet anecdotes abound in the profession of history of missing, faulty, even (dare I breathe it?) apocryphal footnotes. Many—indeed most—are simple errors of transcription;[5] sometimes the writer has no idea how the mistake happened, sometimes publishers simply blew it; sometimes the exigencies of the case demanded a certain creative ingenuity. Such anecdotes are not told with the bravado of hardened criminals and fabricators, but in hushed tones of horror, shame, or embarrassment. The mistakes may be real enough—but they have status as stories precisely because they prick at professional integrity and pride.

But mistakes do not destroy our trust in history, any more than the spelling errors in a cheaply printed classic destroy its standing as great literature. We may bemoan the sloppiness of scholarship, but our sources of trust lie elsewhere. When I read history, I trust *most* the confident, almost unthinking general assertions that could only be made by someone who has steeped themselves in the documents of a particular time and place. When Inga Clendinnen tells us, in a glancing aside, that in the written records of the Spanish Inquisition 'every moan, every whimper, every twist and wrench was meticulously recorded', I have no impulse to demand proof; I do not ask her footnotes to direct me to exemplary details of torture.[6] I accept her assessment because it bears the authority of one who has read it all, who has endured the experience of reading so that she might witness and bear testimony to those sufferings. The unflinching directness of her writing, the complexity of the surrounding argument, bear witness to her scholarship: this is writing driven by conviction, conviction grounded in the experience of reading. I form my contract of trust with the analytic, interpretive, narrative 'voice' of the historian—not with the small change of footnotes.

For historians, the truth will always get in the way of a good story—and make the story better. The creative delights of

history lie in wrestling the intractable fragments into persuasive interpretations that are also good stories. Historians who
delight in writing write inspiringly of 'the struggle of the historian . . . to make the gnomic, refractory remnants of past
sensibilities speak'; of the scope to write with passion and
compassion, or with 'playful imaginative forms' that suit the
shifting grounds of historical realities.[7] Tom Griffiths offers an
extended metaphor of historical writing as clay sculpture: the
careful amassing of the 'raw material of reality', and then, the
paring, sculpting, moulding, tweaking, that is the writer's craft.
'The final reality emerges, and one could almost believe that
it was always there, trapped in the clay, awaiting discovery
and rescue.'[8]

For many years now, my main research project has been
biographical. My reading and writing turn on the particular
complexities of interpreting personality, of locating 'human'
impulses within their constitutive frames of historical circum-
stance and cultural discourse. My primary sources are a woman's diaries;
my self-appointed task to render those diaries into significant
history by analysing them as a permeable interface between
subjectivity and culture. So the character, personality, whims,
aspirations and self-deceptions of my subject—call her Jane—
are central to my interpretation. When I write, I must make
readers accept 'my' Jane as a legitimate, human subject. As a
scholar I am conscious that she is unknowable: or rather, that
I can know her only as a woman formed of words and images,
not of spirit and flesh. But if she remains only an assemblage
of quotations, scattered woodenly across my pages, the intellectual purpose of my work is lost. To make her human, I must
write with a combination of empathy and creativity. For my
book to work, I must 'almost believe' that I know her, inside
and out.

How do I navigate the conflicting pull of intuition and
scepticism, of creativity and evidence? The process of resolution is long and slow, and what disturbs me is how much of it
takes place outside what I think of as the conscious, reasoning

parts of my brain. On first reading one of Jane's diaries, I will transcribe in whole or in part the passages that strike me as bearing significance for my purpose—that are particularly revelatory, or informative. And I transcribe passages in which I find Jane's voice especially engaging, or especially offensive— or when she makes me laugh. Hints and fragments of stories, ideas for interpretation, flicker and form in my head as I read. When I come to write, I read over my compressed collection of interesting and significant passages. New connections and possibilities emerge. The stories drift, coalesce, spawn new twists and turns, and begin to crystallise into sharper, more colourful patterns. As I write, I draw at need from my own notes the most telling quotations. I juxtapose passages initially separated from each other by pages of writing. My role is that of artisan, not of genius: I hew out the jewels, I assemble them in suggestive outlines and patterns, but I do not transform them. I remain a mute presence throughout most of the work, only occasionally pushing in an intrusive authorial voice to tell my reader (still at this stage only myself) what all this might mean.

That's just the first draft. That first draft is a rambling, unsatisfying, unstructured piece of writing. Relationships are signalled but not cemented. The package is wrapped, but the corners poke out. My writing is more assertive than assured, more optimistic than persuasive. But with each ensuing draft I write with rising confidence—that here is a story worthy of telling, that it is true to the life and soul of the voice whose papery whispers first sounded in my head in the archive, that it can now be both liberated and augmented by the addition of my own. In second, third, even fourth rewritings, I sift out the extraneous material. I drop the less significant passages from overlong quotations. I settle my shards of evidence into a more comfortable relationship; I draw more attention to the emerging pattern; I become more relaxed and authoritative in my argument and interpretation. By the final draft I have reduced long blocks of quotation full of dormant meaning to a line or two of assured significance. I have found fragments of new stories lying carelessly scattered through my drafts and honed them into sharply pointed interludes. I write, now, with a sense of full engagement. I am writing inside my head, historical intuition at full stretch, imagination and creativity breathing my chosen significance into a subtle blend of two writing voices: Jane's and my own. No longer do I need to shout from the top of an insecure edifice of archival fragments. I feel assured that the 'truth' of the matter will be revealed in and through the story, produced in my readers' imaginations. I can almost believe it was there all the time.

It is not always possible to return at this point to read the original diary—long, tedious, time-consuming documents that they are, the original (in some cases the only copy) far away on the other side of the world. But when and if I can do so, there is always a sense of shock and readjusted recognition as I come across my favourite, polished, resonant quotations locked snugly back in their original positions. I can find my story in the pages of Jane's diary, certainly—but I find alongside it the thousand other stories that lost their place in mine.

So do I know the difference between fact and fiction? Why is it only at the end of the creative enterprise of writing that I am sure I have 'found' the story that teased and tugged at the edges of my consciousness as I first read her diary? Why is certainty forged on the computer screen and not in the archive where the 'hard evidence', the 'proof', must surely lie? Can I know how much of my certainty derives from my first and subsequent readings of the sources, and how much from the influences of my lived experience, my most recent intellectual encounter, the latest episode of *Neighbours*? Is my writing the product of careful, critical analysis of the evidence of the past, or of my hopelessly compromised and acculturated imagination in the present?

In the grip of creative energy, it is not always possible to discern the precise origin of my interpretations: they feel at once informed and intuitive. Intuition, psychologists will tell us, is not a mystical force but the collation of a thousand hints collected and interpreted subliminally, barely consciously. The more we read one person's diaries, the more we come to feel —perhaps with some justification—that we have a 'hold' on that person's character. In her diaries, Jane's voice rings insistently, forcibly, idiosyncratically. In the cadence of her writing voice, a voice I have immersed myself in for years, I find my strongest points of connection. Here, certainly, I feel the authority of expert knowledge. But my intuitive judgements depend on reactions to her words—imaginative, subjective, empathetic—that are forged in and from my own experience. All this implies something quite disturbing about the truthfulness of history. If, as a historian committed to integrity of purpose and respect for the written record, I still cannot clearly demarcate the subjective from the objective in my own account, what basis do I have to demand my reader's trust?

The solution does not lie in a search and destroy mission, paring out or apologising for every slide into creative engagement. For one thing, to do so would be to produce a history that no one would care to read. Historians have an ethical duty to be readable. They stand witness not only to officially recorded events but to the 'unrecorded' events which have, even so, been trapped in the sprawling and unpredictable mesh of the archives. Only historians, sifting for weeks through dry official records, faded newspapers and forgotten diaries that the rest of the world cares little for, can catch those sideways glimpses that complicate our picture of the past. But if their reportage is as dry and dusty as the archives from which they at last emerge triumphant, will anyone stop to listen?

Imagination is vital to the historian's craft. Without it, the past survives for us only in its inert, tangible form—as scraps of paper and parchment scattered with text and images. With it, the past lives again: not, of course, 'as it really was', and never as if we were really there, but as a living edifice built of fantasy, memory, desire, nostalgia—and knowledge. If we resign the building of that past to the imagination of writers of fiction and film, or to the still more creative imagination of politicians, the edifice becomes a chimera, a site of invention that, if it is not blown away by the first puff of scepticism, is all too vulnerable to strategic reinvention for political purposes. We cannot afford to surrender the appeal to historical imagination, the telling of stories about our past collectivities and past actions, into the hands of popularisers and polemicists whose agenda is so often reactionary and whose politics is all the more insidious because it masquerades as commonsense.

The historian's role is not meaningless reportage, but the production of meaning. We have a duty to bring the more complex stories that lie in the archives to the fore—to engage our readers imaginatively, so they respond with empathy and moral feeling to stories of people who are not immediately 'like themselves'. We need an empathy that crosses the divisions of our multicultural society, not a comfortable, closed recognition and reassurance that will enfix and naturalise them. If I deny myself a place in my analysis, I destroy the only base from which I can attempt to understand. 'There has to be a bit of ourselves in the writing', writes Griffiths. 'That's where we start'. And, perhaps, where we finish.[9]

Can we license imagination without edging into dishonesty? The answer may lie in 'intellectual play', or a more visible presence of the historian's 'needle I' in the writing.[10] Great writers can manage this brilliantly. But in clumsier hands such performative, self-conscious strategies can seem intrusive or unbalanced. Most of us read history to learn something of the past, not to admire the performance of the historian. When I read, I am more often repelled than beguiled by a historian who interrupts history with reflections on his or her own craft.

I'd like to think there was a more subtle way of achieving the same end. Vanden Bossche writes of Thomas Carlyle that his faith that his 'open loving heart' could discern the truth of another human being was continually troubled by his recognition that all that really remained to him was a mixed bag of tattered remnants that had once clothed an external figure.

Carlyle, posits Bossche, reconciled that conflict, so familiar to all historians, by the artfulness of his writing. He never expounded uncertainty—far from it. The sweep of Carlyle's authoritiative pronouncements echo across the centuries, by turns chilling, compelling, and heartwarming. But they echo in his own distinctive voice, a voice imbued with theatricality and self-evident art. Carlyle's truths are compellingly presented—but we never for a moment forget that they are Carlyle's.[11]

Grace Cossington Smith claimed that she only painted what she saw.[12] As historians, we must tell what we find. But what we find is inevitably distinctive, individual, political and personal. We read the unknowable past through the intimate knowledge we have of ourselves: we interpret through our own experience, responding to the archives with our own embodied sense of justice, humanity, anger and love. Perhaps the most vital art of historical narrative is to keep it free from ponderous qualifications or abstract reflections on Truth—but still to write in a way that embeds in our history the recognition that this is one story, my story, this story I am telling you, from which you may forge your own. And yet that captures the intensity of Carlyle's conviction: 'The Thing which I here hold imaged in my mind did actually occur.'[13] I'm telling you stories. Trust me.[14]

NOTES

[1]   E. L. Gilbert, 'Rescuing reality: Carlyle, Froude, and biographical truth-telling', *Victorian Studies*, vol. 34, no. 3, Spring, 1991, pp. 302–3.

[2]   Stuart Macintyre, 'History, politics and the philosophy of history', *Australian Historical Studies*, vol. 35, no. 123, April, 2004, p. 132.

[3]   Inga Clendinnen, 'Fellow sufferers: History and imagination', *Australian Humanities Review*, vol. 3, September 1996, http://www.lib.latrobe.edu.au/AHR/archive/Issue-Sept-1996/clendinnen.html; Tom Griffiths, 'Essaying the truth', *Meanjin*, vol. 59, no. 1, 2000, p. 136.

4   Griffiths, 'Essaying the truth', p. 143.
5   Macintyre, on the basis of experience, estimates that errors creep in at a rate of one in ten. 'History, politics and the philosophy of history', p. 133.
6   Clendinnen, 'Fellow sufferers'.
7   Clendinnen, 'Fellow sufferers'; Cassandra Pybus, 'Response to Inga Clendinnen', *Australian Humanities Review*, vol. 3, September 1996, http://www.lib.latrobe.edu.au/AHR/emuse/History/pybus.htm.
8   Griffiths, 'Essaying the truth', p. 136.
9   Griffiths, 'Essaying the truth', p. 133.
10 Clendinnen, 'Fellow sufferers'; Pybus, 'Response'.
11 C. R. Vanden Bossche, 'Fictive text and transcendental self: Carlyle's art of biography', *Biography*, vol. 10, no. 2, 1987, pp. 119, 125–6.
12 Drusilla Modjeska, *Stravinsky's Lunch*, Picador, Sydney, 1999, p. 205.
13 Thomas Carlyle, 'Biography' (1832), *Critical and Miscellaneous Essays*, vol. III, Chapman and Hall, London, 1899, p. 54.
14 The narrators' refrain in Jeanette Winterson's *The Passion* (Penguin, London, 1988). On Winterson's pertinence for historiography, see C. Brockmann, ' "Trust me, I'm (not) telling you stories." Historiography, fiction and Jeanette Winterson', BA(Hons) thesis (History), University of Sydney, 2003.

CHAPTER 10

FIONA PAISLEY

DISCOVERIES MADE IN
THE ARCHIVES

In her recent account of historical archives and their limitations, the historian of gender and the British Empire Antoinette Burton asserts that official records are necessarily partial and fallible—they are themselves the products of history. She counsels that the unreliability of the archives should not cause us to despair. Rather, this realisation helps us comprehend, she argues, an important and productive point: any relationship we establish with historical sources necessarily entangles our own interests and concerns in the present. Conversely, this entanglement illuminates the ways in which historical relations continue to shape our lives. In particular, Burton notes that imperial and colonial histories continue to influence how, why, and what history is written. Reflecting on the incompleteness of archival material, given the legacies of these individual and collective historical conditions, Burton concludes that 'the ultimate fragmentation and ghostliness of all archives . . . [is] the final unknowability of home and history in their totalities'.[1]

While rectifying the archival silences of history represents a significant ethical issue facing many historians today, my concern here rests with the opposite problem: how to ethically respond to the often voluminous controversial, painful, or offensive archival sources pertaining to minority groups. I take Burton's insight as a starting point from which to think about the question of my own relationship to the archives. My focus is on assimilation, those policies directed towards Aboriginal women, men, and children emerging as fully fledged state and federal government objectives in the first half of the twentieth century. And my interest is in the 'discoveries' made not only of 'the past' but also of my place in the history of assimilation as lived in the present.

Assimilation is and continues to be a subject of debate between historians. While most view assimilation as both a set of policies and a foundational narrative central to settler colonialism itself, differences between Indigenous and non-Indigenous historians are most evident in terms of balancing the relationship between the two. During the closing discussion at a conference on the topic of assimilation held in 2001 at the University of Sydney, this double history of assimilation quickly became a matter of contention. Numbers of Indigenous participants questioned the wisdom of the relatively narrow focus adopted by many of the conference papers presented by non-Indigenous historians. Where the majority of Indigenous commentators emphasised that assimilation began at the point of first colonisation and continued to the present day, they expressed concern that non-Indigenous historians tended to periodise assimilation as an official policy emerging most fully in the post-World War II era. I do not wish to imply that the views expressed at this conference should be understood to reflect those held by the diversity of Indigenous and non-Indigenous historians engaged in writing about assimilation in its various forms. Nonetheless, the intensity of the Indigenous intervention that day reminded me once again

of the very real and present stakes for groups differently constituted by history. Learning from this criticism, it is apparent
that remembering that the past has powerfully present political significance, with enormous implication for the historian's
relationship to her or his chosen archives, wherever and whatever they may be.

Biographies, oral histories and family histories increasingly
supplement the partial perspectives of official records where
minority histories are little represented, yet they too are fallible
and demand our critical attention. Whether official and formal
or personal, communal, and informal, historical sources share
more similarities than usually acknowledged. Not least, they
share a remarkable capacity for leaving out, overlooking, and,
in some cases, suppressing, the past as much as informing us
about it. Connecting the two, our autobiographical and family
archives come into play in the kinds of historical projects we
engage in as historians. Imperial and colonial histories have
not been distant from my family history although their Australian inflexion has become more apparent to me only in
adult life. Although I was born in Scotland to Scottish parents,
my mother was born in Sri Lanka and enjoyed there as a small
child the imperial twilight years of the 1930s. She remembers
her ayah and a life more in common with *The Secret Garden*
than might be expected of the interwar generation. Travelling
to Australia with her husband and young children in the 1960s
must have been a kind of return to the colonies, if in a modern
guise. In other intergenerational traces, my family's fragmented
photograph archive includes an intriguing snapshot of the
imperial late nineteenth century. On the veranda of a colonial
bungalow sit members of a clearly wealthy family, their Indian
servants by the steps. No one in our family remembers who
these people are or what they are doing in our family photo
collection.

And in my own lifetime, recently arrived from England in
the early 1970s, I spent my early teenage years in Nowra, a
coastal town in New South Wales. As I struggled to understand

my new world, I dutifully learned the names of flying doctors
and the dates of leper colonies, and painted sunset-lit outback
landscapes by following the example of my classmates. Other
mysteries in my new life were however less easily solved. For
example, what nationality was the dark-skinned man who
sometimes arrived at the end of the day to collect a boy in my
class? I was unable to connect this school friend with the
fictional Aboriginal boy who played with his white friend in
'The Rocks of Honey', the serialised version of Patricia
Wrightson's book we read each week in the school magazine.
Unlike his fictional counterpart, my schoolmate was freckle-
faced and not mysterious or shy at all. Later, much later, I
wondered where the other Aboriginal children in our part of
town went to school. Indeed, where was the Aboriginal population in Nowra? It seems hard to believe now, but over the
four years I spent there, I remained ignorant of this significant
local knowledge. As historian Peter Read has so hauntingly
described, it is a legacy of the history of colonisation and
assimilation that non-Indigenous people can occupy the same
space as Indigenous communities and not 'see' them.[2] Only
retrospectively have I been able to situate my school years in
Nowra in the early 1970s within the history of Indigenous
child removal in New South Wales. I know through my
research that Bomaderry, where I attended high school for
two years, and specifically the local Cootamundra Girls Home,
was one of the most notorious of dispersal points of Aboriginal children removed into institutions and then service in
Australian history.

  While such traces indicate that I am one of a long line of
Scottish immigrants to the colonies, unlike previous generations I feel no residing loyalty for the Old Country. My historical research speaks of a desire to find instead an ethical way
to be an Anglo-Celtic Australian settler colonial. In 1990 I
began research for my doctoral thesis to investigate national
and international campaigns to challenge assimilation made by
Anglo-Australian women. Over following years, I was struck

by the ambivalent status they mobilised as settler colonial women seeking to promote Indigenous rights within the British Commonwealth. While they expressed a desire for a settler colonialism that would include the rights of Indigenous people, they did so on the basis of their asserted responsibility as white women of the British Commonwealth to speak for 'the Aborigines'. Ironically, the heartfelt if problematic articulations of a humanitarian agenda they made are echoed in my own determination to write their history, a sobering and instructive interface between past and present if ever there was one.

Reflecting on my choice of research subjects, I have come to the conclusion that the relationship between the projects historians select and the questions that emerge as fundamental to their lives are intimately connected, suggesting a fascinating if little discussed symbiosis. The evident inseparability of our selves from history might form the basis for our comprehension of even the most official of archives as remarkably contemporary places rather than merely repositories of the past. Although they might seem like dusty places out of the way of the world, official records (for example, concerning Aboriginal policy and administration) contain within them decisions that not only have impacted upon individual lives but also have sought to govern the futures of whole peoples. Award-winning historian Anna Haebich has documented the institutionalisation of Aboriginal children removed for training towards their 'absorption' into the larger community through intensive archival research in Western Australia, and more recently in a national account encompassing research in state and federal archives across Australia. Her work illustrates the ways in which intensive historical research is complemented by compassion and sometimes bewilderment. How can it be that these things happen, she asks, even as she offers her own carefully considered answers?[3]

Like many of my colleagues working in Aboriginal history archives, this material continues to shock and disturb me. On more than one occasion, I have turned the page in a file to be confronted by the account of some dreadful event too horrible to recount. While non-Indigenous access to sensitive material concerning Aboriginal people has been rightly restricted, in many cases what is generally available still raises important questions about disclosure. One example of my decision to withhold information concerns an account written by a conscience-stricken contemporary of the horrific torture and murder of an Aboriginal woman being brought into Darwin in the 1930s. Brought under police guard to give evidence at the trial of an Aboriginal man, she suffered terrible humiliations over a number of days. After reading about her death, I felt a strong sense of responsibility to give a posthumous voice to this woman. Yet I have never been able to write up my research notes, still finding the material too disturbing to shape into any formal narrative.

Less starkly, perhaps, but still as traumatising, various kinds of violence recorded in the archives reinscribe Indigenous people as the objects of history. While engagement with historical material of this nature necessarily implicates the historian in the very settler colonial relations she or he may seek to illuminate, unfortunately, in order to illustrate the implications of assimilation, for example, it is necessary to provide graphic evidence of its dreadful power. What better example than the case of the Western Australian Chief Protector's own account of his pro-absorption vision. In 1947, A. O. Neville's *Australia's Coloured Minority* included photographic evidence purporting to document his mission to save the Aboriginal people from themselves—a series of highly offensive and distressing 'before and after' testimonials to his own benevolence. These images paired children, the 'bush waifs' he claimed to have discovered alone and unprotected, with later photographs of their grown-up selves, women who smile for the camera as they live under his 'protection'.[4] The immediate question for a historian is under what circumstances were these images taken? Their subjects could little have had little premonition of the captions that would assert their proportion of 'white' blood as sign of their ascendance into civilisation. Should such images be used by historians in seeking to explain the implications of biological absorption promoted by Neville and others among his peers? On one hand, the reproduction of these images offers opportunities for the circulation of his vision undreamed of by Neville himself. On the other, those who appear in them are unnamed—types mobilised in an account of their own demise as members of a race. Despite these concerns, I reproduced Neville's photographs in my thesis and later my book. I have used them also to illustrate various conference papers and when lecturing students— always taking great care to provide them with the necessary historical context. My aim was to honour the untold story of those people so captured in photographs as they had been taken away and institutionalised in real life, though I was never fully persuaded by my own argument.

Despite disjunctures of the sort I have described above that litter our histories, personal and collective, history contains within it nonetheless the potential to allow for new exchanges in the present. Thus Australian historian Heather Goodall points out that shared space in itself provides the grounds for writing about histories of place and identity across historically distanced communities, and to find surprising parallels in attachments to place, objects, and memories.[5] Such was my feeling when I read Stephen Kinnane's new book *Shadow Lines*. Kinnane is an Indigenous writer who has spent a great deal of time in the archives. As Kinnane points out, Aboriginal people (including members of his own family) who have read material from the official archives have been profoundly shocked by the information kept by Neville's department, material purporting to provide factual accounts of their daily lives, but routinely incorrect and often slanderous, petty and cruel. Kinnane's book brilliantly reminds us that the archive on assimilation finds its larger meaning in the memories, community, and life stories of its subjects. In this case, Noongar women Aunty Eileen Harwood, Aunty Mary Cross and Aunty Elsie Gardiner are invited by Kinnane to discuss the photographs taken of themselves as children and young women and used by Neville in his notorious book.[6] In the process, these stolen pictures, the ones I had guiltily reproduced, were reunited with their subjects.

Researching the history of Aboriginal policy in the inter-war years has profoundly shaped my relationship to the archives and to Australian history more generally. But it has also shaped my understanding of my own positionality as an Anglo-Australian. Over the years, I have been engaged in projects with evident parallels in my own desires as a historian to think about a way forward in the present. This is one of the discoveries I have made in the archives, mundane perhaps, but a discovery nonetheless.

NOTES

[1] Antoinette Burton, 'Archive fever and the panoptican of history', in Burton, *Dwelling in the Archives: Women Writing House, Home, and History in Late Colonial India*, Oxford University Press, New York, 2003, p. 144.
[2] Peter Read, *Belonging: Australians, Place and Aboriginal Ownership*, Cambridge University Press, Cambridge, 2000, especially chapter 8.
[3] Anna Haebich, *Broken Circles: Fragmenting Indigenous Families 1800–2000*, Fremantle Arts Centre Press, Fremantle, WA, 2000.
[4] A. O. Neville, *Australia's Coloured Minority: Its Place in the Community*, Currawong, Sydney, 1947.
[5] Heather Goodall, 'Too early yet or not soon enough? Reflections on sharing histories as process', *Australian Historical Studies*, vol. 33, no. 118, 2002, pp. 7–24.
[6] Stephen Kinnane, *Shadow Lines*, Fremantle Arts Centre Press, Fremantle, WA, 2003, pp. 270ff.

GLENDA SLUGA

WHOSE HISTORY?

Every nation has its 'history wars', contentious debates about the past, what happened and why it is still important. The past, after all, is intrinsic to the idea of nationhood. But what if those debates, and the rancour they invite, don't recognise national borders? I offer what follows as a reflection on this question, the role it has played in my own historical writing, and its implications for thinking about what gets written and discussed about the past in Australia.

Struggles over the meaning of the past are not just the stuff of ivory towers. They occur in the most unexpected places. Their participants are as likely to be toolmakers, milkbar owners, grandmothers and the unemployed as academics and journalists. History is a public discourse. Any society has more than one public. Readers of the *Age* might also read the *Sydney Morning Herald*, and even the *Australian*, but that doesn't mean they read *Neos Kosmos* or *Cosmopolitan*. They may watch SBS and the ABC, but that doesn't mean they see *Live at Five*, watch *Al-Jazeera* or hear the morning news in Mandarin. Neither do they all talk to the same people. Those that hang out at the local RSL will probably not visit a Croatian Club at any time in their life. But they can expect that in any Croatian club they visit within Australia a portrait will be hanging of Ante Pavelic, the leader of the Independent State of Croatia from 1941 to 1945, and hero of Croatian nationalism.

The historical controversy that surrounds Pavelic and his portrait is not that apparent to everyone who attends an Australian Croatian club. In the western suburbs of Melbourne there is a Croatian club erected in the 1970s in Pavelic's name. The club recently abandoned that name for political reasons, although Pavelic's portrait still hangs on the wall. Not that the name matters to everyone. I have relatives, who are not Croatian, who have visited that club on the invitation of friends, or extended family members who hold functions there and have to be reminded that Pavelic was an ally of German forces in World War II, and they hardly seem to care, even though their own family members fought against Germany and its fascist allies. They do not remember that it was Pavelic who ran the nationalist paramilitary organisation known as the Ustasha, or that he is associated in some historical contexts with genocidal acts against Serbs. That past does not seem to matter to them. However, in a provocative study on transnational nationalisms, the sociologist Zlatko Skrbis shows that, for many 'second generation' Croatians who have visited these clubs, the past, and its controversies, do still matter, just as they do currently in Croatia itself.[1]

The portraits of Pavelic suggest that at least some migrants who left newly communist Yugoslavia in the postwar years thought of their freedom in Australia, at least partly, in terms of being able to lay claim to a Croatian identity through an identification with Pavelic and what he stood for—or their historical version of what he stood for, which may not coincide with the version I have offered here. However, Skrbis suggests that Pavelic's portraits, like the statues of Draza Mihajlovic—the leader of Serb Royalists known as Cetniks who fought the Ustasha (sometimes on the side of the Germans, sometimes against them)—perched outside Australian Serb Orthodox churches, is disconcerting for the children of those same people. While still interested in their Croatian identification, they have taken issue with the status Pavelic has sustained. In other words, there is, within Australian political borders, a controversy over the meaning of Croatian identity, which has as its focus interpretations of the past, and its present significance. This controversy involves questions of guilt, genocide, and victimhood, it is very real among a specific community, but it has almost no place in the Australian academy, or in Australian media. It lives its own secret life on the web, in folklore and anecdote, and in imported publications. And it is rarely engaged by local (nationally based) historians, and, as a result, lacks any local academic critique.

The omnipresence of portraits of Pavelic allows me to trace the *transnational* nature of nationalisms and of histories, and of their crooked reach. When applied to Australian society, the idea of transnationalism, (not unlike multiculturalism) can seem somewhat hackeneyed. When applied to the study of Australian history, it is almost incongruous, except in the arena of migration history—most usually the history of immigration to Australia.

My first book, *Bonegilla: A Place of No Hope*, was about the Bonegilla 'reception centre', which operated from 1947 until 1971 as a migrant processing centre. I took it up while searching for a topic for my Masters degree in History. My father had been to Bonegilla briefly, a play had been written about it, and its history had yet to be researched in any substantial way.[2] Bonegilla was a place where immigrants brought out under the auspices of the Australian government's postwar 'populate or perish' immigration scheme were to be Australianised, taught the English language and 'the Australian way of life'. The latter equated to lessons in hygiene and housekeeping for the female immigrants. Over the period of its operation more than 300 000 people passed through the Bonegilla camp for periods varying from a few days to ten years.

In its early days, a time when refugees were happily referred to as migrants or reffos, Bonegilla's distance from Albury (eight miles), the nearest town, and from any of the main urban centres (at least a six-hour train journey), was considered adequate by the Australian government for meeting the conditions of its improvised immigration policy, including the notion of 'dispersal' and non-confrontation with local populations. Migrants who had exchanged two years of their labour for assisted or free passage could be railed from Bonegilla to remote areas of the Australian continent, to be placed in jobs Anglo-Australians did not want to do, often out in the bush, with inadequate shelter. At Bonegilla they could be stratified into social and occupational classifications, as new Australians, as labourer if male, or domestic if female, regardless of their educational qualifications and skills. It is this aspect of Bonegilla's function (realising and reinforcing an ethnically segmented and stratified labour force) that left its imprint on the lives of the majority of those who passed through. Mainstream narratives of Australian history ignore the existence not only of Bonegilla, but also of two major riots that occurred there in 1952 and 1961, the consequences of economic recession and of the uncompromising and patronising attitudes of the Australian authorities.

In writing about Bonegilla I was particularly interested in the contrast between its ongoing life in the migration memories of a whole range of immigrants to Australia, even those who had never been there, and its marginality, if not invisibility, in surveys of Australian history. It was that history that alerted me to the fact that 'historiographical attempts to incorporate migrants as political and social actors into the mainstream of Australian history, as citizens reshaping and redefining Australian history as well as its society have been few'.[3] Australia *is* a transnational society, but those experiences hardly register in mainstream historiography and its themes. These focus on race relations in terms of white and black (and to a lesser extent yellow), and on the relationship between British-based and indigenous cultures. Migration history sits outside those dichotomies.[4] Perhaps it is the analysts of the current political controversies over refugee policy and asylum seekers who will note, and ponder, the lack of controversy about or interest in the transnational past.

The transnational nature of national histories has other faces. One belongs to the Australian-based historian involved in off-shore controversies, which the multicultural nature of modern societies inevitably brings home. My second book, *The Problem of Trieste and the Italo-Yugoslav Border*, embroiled me in the controversies that have raged in the Adriatic region of Europe around the histories of Italian fascism, of communism and the Cold War, and the nature of nations and national identity.[5] My contribution was an account of the role of race-thinking and stereotypes in the international attempts to resolve the political and historical debates regarding Italy's north-eastern border over the course of the twentieth century. Since the end of World War I, Trieste has been part of Italy; before then it was the main trading port for the Austro-Hungarian empire. But over this same period that border shifted, just as the nature of its two imbricated states had changed. In the early twentieth century the border isolated a Fascist Italy from a Yugoslav Kingdom; in the latter half of that century it distanced a liberal Italian republic and the non-communist west from a communist (non-aligned) Yugoslavia, and its Soviet satellite communist neighbours; at the twenty-first century it links Italy to the new nation-state of Slovenia in a European Union. Historians writing about the region, some of them local but many from elsewhere, had promoted the view that the problem of

Trieste was a consequence of its diversity, and of the allegedly
fundamental cultural differences between Italian-speakers they
stereotyped as western, and Slovene and Croatian-speakers
racialised as Slavs and 'Balkan'. My purpose in writing the
Trieste book was to reclaim for history the ambiguity of identity in the Adriatic boundary region, and to incorporate voices
which did not fit into the neat categorisations of ethnic, political and gender identities assumed in historical arguments for
ethnically homogenous forms of national sovereignty. The
book received strong reviews outside Italy, in German newspapers, and English-language journals. But my efforts earned
me the adjective 'slavophile' from self-consciously Italian colleagues; among historians of the Cold War, I was an apologist
for Stalin. The fact that my parents were bilingual Italian–
Slovene speakers from the Trieste region, that my surname
was 'Sluga' (a slavic term for a tithed or unwaged servant), *and*
that I was from Australia, certainly did not help. For a critical
Italian audience, being Australian explains my insensitivity to
narratives about the historical legacy of a long and deep ethno-
national civilisation.

In the context of the history of the Trieste region, my
interest in unsettling the validity of ethnic and racial stereotypes about Italians and 'Slavs', and the relationship between
them, meant giving some space to the concept of 'brotherhood'
promoted by local communists and their fellow travellers from
the latter stages of World War II. In the interwar period, when
the Trieste region lay within Italian borders, Fascist policies
had discriminated against and harassed not only communists,
but bilingual Italian citizens, and thrived on a rhetoric of anti-
Slavism that associated communism with Slavs. After the col-
lapse of the Italian Fascist government in September 1943, local
anti-Fascists (a mixture of Slovenes/Italians and communists/
non-communists from the Trieste region and Croatian-
speaking Istria) increasingly favoured inclusion of their region
in a future communist Yugoslavia as a means of liberating the

population from the burden of the Fascist past, and in the name of 'Italo-Slovene brotherhood'. In May 1945 these pro-Yugoslav anti-Fascist 'partisans' took credit for liberating Trieste from the Nazi occupiers and for installing a new 'Italo-Slovene' administration there. I was interested in the impulse that drove some of the individuals involved to repel the chauvinist politics that had taken hold under Fascism, and in their conscious, albeit awkward, attempts to recapture a notion of a culturally diverse (if ideologically uniform!) community. I was also interested in how their non-nationalist rhetoric was identified as suspicious and a threat to democratic order by British and American Allied forces operating in the same region.

When in June 1945 the British-American Allied forces took control of the Trieste region from the 'partisans' in order to oversee international discussions of the geo-political future of the contested territory, they supported allegations made by the pro-Italian groups that during the war and at its end the pro-Yugoslav partisans driven by ethnic hatred rather than anti-Fascist rancour had killed Italians and buried their bodies in deep natural caverns along the Adriatic coastline. Local historians have continued to debate (often with great vitriol) the existence of these mass graves and their victims and perpetrators. At the same time, the theme of the mass graves—known as *foibe*—and the proposition that individuals who can be collectively identified as 'Slavs' practiced a form of genocide against Italians (whether Fascist or not) has grown in political significance since the end of the Cold War, and since the break up of Yugoslavia.

In the context of Italian historiography, the end of the Cold War has invited historical revisionism and a growing critique of not only communism, but the left in general. This critique has opened the space for a celebration of conservatism and the right, which has redefined all anti-communism as good politics, even when exercised in fascist forms. Baldly speaking, on this 'post-fascist' view, Italian Fascism was patriotic given

the threat to the Italian state posed by communism and its
Slavic imperative. On this view too, communist Italians, who
in the twentieth century exerted an influence in Western
Europe greater than any other national Communist party,
were by virtue of their ideology traitors and, in the Trieste
region, most probably not Italians.

From the 1990s the convergence of the shift in popular
and academic historical narratives about World War II, and the
violent breakup of Yugoslavia, has encouraged some Italian
government ministers to draw on the historical narratives of
genocide and ethnic cleansing in the Trieste region (by Slavs
against Italians) for their own political purposes. Among those
purposes are claims to reparations for the loss of territory including Trieste and extending down the Istrian coastline into
modern-day Croatia, a terrain which some nationalists still
regard as Italy's by right of history and language.[6] Into the turmoil of this historical ring, I threw my argument that given
the cultural and ideological complexity of local identities and
relationships, assumptions about ethnic hatred between Italians
and Slavs were unhelpful, and constituted, at the least, bad
history.

Historians and their historical narratives have had an important role in the representations of places and people, and
the reproduction of national identities and boundaries. Historians, like nationalists, have tended to idealise the political
and cultural homogeneity of national communities, in the past
as well as the present, particularly at times of national political
crisis. Indeed, there is a close relationship between the ways in
which groups (such as Italians and Slavs, Australians and
migrants, Aborigines, or Asians) are 'imaginatively' represented
in academic and popular histories, and the power or authority
individuals interpellated into those groups are able to exercise.
J. G. A. Pocock argues that historical narratives (versions of
the past and representations of identities in the past) are potent
attributes of sovereignty, since they are used to identify and

determine the (national) limits or borders of a political entity's affairs.[7] But is it the historian's job to unify and homogenise what was or is disparate and diverse?

Among the Allied soldiers of the British Eighth Army who were brought in to confront the pro-Yugoslav forces in Trieste in May 1945, and finally took over from them, were Maori troops from New Zealand, and a battalion of Indian Ghurkhas. While their superiors stressed the linguistic and cultural foreignness and 'Moor-like' faces of 'Slavs', the official histories of these battalions note that Maoris and Gurkhas actually spent a lot of time singing, dancing, and 'fraternising' with the partisans. Certainly some of the Maori Battalion had cultural connections with the Croatians in the local forces. Croatian-speakers from the Dalmatian coast were among the most distinctive of migrants to New Zealand and had married among the indigenous population. There were rumours too that the Gurkhas were amenable to the partisans' talk of overthrowing all forms of cultural oppression, an argument that may have appealed given the fragile political status of the Indian sub-continent.

The transnational rumblings of this history, its enmities and alliances, coincidences and convergences, do not end there. After the war, Australian immigration officials were stationed in Trieste in search of suitable immigrants to populate its nether regions, and provide much needed labour. The ships that left Trieste when the Italian government finally resumed authority in the region in 1954 took 'migrants' to Bonegilla. Among them was my father, escaping conscription and what seemed to him the hopelessness of life in the new communist Yugoslavia, and my mother, seeking my father. Whose history should I write and for whom? Is the transnational and multi-cultural nature of history only of concern to me because I am the embodiment of an Australian experience of both those

terms? Maybe the relative silence in Australia in regard to
many historical controversies is as it should be, particularly
given the very immediate social, political, and economic issues
at stake in the race concerns of the 'history war' in Australia.
Certainly no one would argue that Italian-based historians
must take notice of Australian indigenous and colonial (or
even communist) history. And when Italian historians do set
their minds to that history, who takes any notice here? Or are
all histories, and thus all historical controversies, interrelated?

The relevance of the Croatian example (which is one I
know of particularly) to the transnational model of historiography hit home about ten years ago when the 'history wars'
in Yugoslavia transformed into a series of real wars. The phil-
ologist Svetlana Slapsak, once of the Insitute of Art and Literature at Belgrade University, now a teacher at the University of
Ljubljana in independent Slovenia, described the process this
way: 'Imaginary Chetniks and Ustasha were again and again
invented until they finally "materialised" in paramilitary units.
The aim of the surrealistic movement, so important in Serbian
literature, has been realised: literature has come to life.'[8] Slapsak
blamed the destruction of Yugoslavia and its 'multinational
and multicultural society' not on an abstract nationalism,
but on 'words called up and sent out into the public domain
by intellectuals'. Other commentators noted the role of the
'diaspora' connected to specific lines of patronage and community, and displaced from the complexity of the local situation. Significantly, historical wars had became real wars
because of the irresponsibility of, among others, historians
(Franjo Tudjman, the leader of the Croatian state which did
not formally identify with Pavelic, but some of whose supporters did, was an historian). To some degree, the new wars
between (depending on when and where) individuals whose
motives were reduced to their collective assignations as Serbs
or Croats or 'Muslims' or Bosnians or Albanians or Macedo-
nians, were conceived of, or imagined, with the help of commentators in the press and on television, as well as in the

universities, as extensions of older wars. But they were also wars fought to affirm a particular version of those past wars and of past and present injustices. The sides that coalesced into ethno-religious groupings did so as a result of the ways in which historical narratives were invoked. The wars were fuelled not so much by an absence of historical discourses, but by 'the destruction of the balance in public discourse' through 'the invention of collective enemies for collective national entities'.[9]

While the wars in Yugoslavia were taking place in the early 1990s I was teaching a course on Contemporary Europe in the History Department at the University of Sydney. There was no way to ignore the conflict. It became impossible to lecture on its historical background and significance without being caught up in the turbulence of feelings—whether among Croatian, Serbian, Macedonian, Bosnian, Greek, or other students. Some students were refugees from the conflict, fresh from Sarajevo or Tuzla in Bosnia. Some were the 'second generation migrants' who had rediscovered the relevance of the images of Pavelic or Mihajlovic at their local Croat or Serbian community centre. Some may even have once expressed their unease about those images. But now it was as if they had no way of contesting or taking up these 'history wars' in any substantial way. The absence of informed historical commentary or debate was in this context haunting. Certainly it was my task to offer them a sense of that debate. Given that some male members of that same student body volunteered to spend their summer vacations fighting in the real wars that were then raging around them, albeit in long-distance form within the borders of another political nation, I cannot imagine but that my efforts were inconsequential.

The question of the ethics of history writing raises the problem of the overlapping and parallel layers of history wars, and

the portability and mutuality of national histories. If all func-
tional societies have multiple publics and foster multiple historical narratives, what is the responsibility of the historian?
Whose history and which war should they engage? Do all historians working in Australia have a responsibility to engage in
some way the question of Aboriginal genocide and 'black-
armband history'? These historical debates about Australia's
black past are most prominent currently. They are certainly
most consequential for communities that have been disadvan-
taged not only by the 'whitewashing' of history, but also by
the established mores of a discipline that disallows the validity
and legitimacy of their own past experiences. Or should the
historian regardless of where they live only speak for the historical debates of the community or nation in which they
specialise, whether it be Belgian or Hutu? Whatever the
possible answers to these questions, certainly the moral of the
Yugoslav wars is that historians who disregard their ethical
responsibility towards the past, towards its complexities (as
often of a transnational as national, and popular as professional
kind) may have responsibility for real wars. What one expects
and would hope for is a phalanx of engaged historians, not on
a warpath, but committed to airing and discussing subjects
that are deemed taboo, whether because of the aggressive
emotions to which they may give rise, or because of the challenge they pose to national forms of identity and culture otherwise maintained through transnational means.

NOTES

[1] See Zlatko Skrbis, *Long Distance Nationalism: Diasporas, Homelands,
and Identities*, Ashgate, Aldershot, 1999.

[2] See in particular, Richard Bosworth, who was one of the first
historians in Australia to probe its transnational past: Richard
Bosworth and Janis Wilton, *Old Worlds and New Australia: The Post-
war Migrant Experience*, Penguin, Ringwood, 1984; and Richard

Bosworth and Romano Uglini (eds), *War Internment, and Mass Migration, the Italo-Australian Experience, 1940–1990*, Gruppo Editoriale Internazionale, Roma, 1992.

3   See Glenda Sluga, 'Bonegilla and migrant dreaming', in Kate Darian-Smith and Paula Hamilton, *Memory and History in Twentieth Century Australia*, Oxford University Press, Melbourne, 2004, p. 208.

4   See Sara Wills' more recent argument, in 'Un-stitching the lips of migrant nation', *Australian Historical Studies,* vol. 33, no. 118, 2002, special issue: *Challenging Histories*, pp. 71–89.

5   See Glenda Sluga, *The Problem of Trieste: Difference, Identity and Sovereignty in Twentieth-Century Europe*, State University of New York Press, Albany, 2001.

6   Italy had officially gained that territory in 1921 and lost it in 1954 after a series of failed attempts to gain an international resolution to its contest with Communist Yugoslavia.

7   J. G. A. Pocock, 'The politics of history: The subaltern and the subversive', *Journal of Political Philosophy*, vol. 6, no. 3, 1998, pp. 219–34.

8   Svetlana Slapsak, 'Serbian alternatives: Are there any?', *East European Reporter*, Sept./Oct. 1992, p. 54. Slapsak was dismissed from Belgrade University for opposing the imprisonment of an Albanian political prisoner from Kosovo.

9   Slapsak, 'Serbian alternatives', p. 53.

CHAPTER 12

DAVID CHRISTIAN

HISTORY AND
GLOBAL IDENTITY

Mma Ramotswe thought: God put us on this earth. We were all
Africans then, in the beginning, because man started in Kenya, as
Dr Leakey and his Daddy have proved. So, if one thinks carefully
about it, we are all brothers and sisters, and yet everywhere you
look, what do you see? Fighting, fighting, fighting. Rich people
killing poor people; poor people killing rich people. Everywhere,
except Botswana.[1]

By a 'global identity', I mean a sense of belonging to the
global community of humans that can inspire collective action
as powerfully as modern nationalisms. The question this essay
raises is simple to state but difficult to answer: is such a sense
of global identity possible? Is it possible that people throughout the world may eventually learn to identify with the community of all human beings, past and present, as they do now
with their national, religious, or ethnic communities? If so, can
the sense of a shared humanity ever generate the depth of feeling and the sense of shared purpose and self-sacrifice that
nation states have so often called on in times of war?

139

The question is profoundly important because, as globalisation forces different communities into uncomfortable inti-
macy, while military technologies become more destructive,
and global problems more urgent, the absence of a sense of
global identity will increase the likelihood of catastrophic
conflict, while reducing the likelihood of finding shared solutions to global problems. This essay will concentrate on the
role historians may play in constructing (or failing to construct)
a sense of global identity.

A sense of community seems to be inescapable in a social
species such as our own. Knowing what community you
belong to is part of your self-identity; it tells you who you are,
who you can trust, who are your friends and who are your
enemies. As a result, a sense of community can motivate people
at very deep levels. But the sense of community is rarely
simple. Particularly in complex societies such as those of the
modern world, identities are variable, overlapping and multiple. Individuals identify themselves as members of many different communities—those of family, gender, class, work place,
or sporting team—and in any particular situation, they draw on
the identity that is most appropriate. Each community shapes
our sense of identity and the way we act.

Though nationalism provides just one of the many different identities available in the modern world, nationalist identities have proved to be peculiarly powerful. As Ross Poole
puts it:

> The modern world provides many different cultural forms and
> associated identities which cut across, complement or conflict with
> the nation and its identity. Nonetheless, the nation has asserted its
> priority over other cultural forms, most obviously in its claim to a
> political embodiment. It is the nation—not religion, political prin-
> ciple, local community, or social class—which demands its own
> state. And it could not sustain this claim to priority unless national
> identity was experienced as more fundamental than others. At least
> part of the reason for this is that the nation has appropriated to

itself the basic means of self-expression and communication. The very means by which individuals form a conception of who they are defines them as members of a specific nation.[2]

Indeed, so strong are the claims that nationalism makes on individuals that many millions of people have sacrificed their lives more or less willingly to defend the nation states with which they identify.

For most modern governments, nationalism offers a powerful way of unifying and mobilising millions of people. This is particularly apparent in wartime of course, but it is also apparent in times of peace. As a cohesive force, nationalism has undoubtedly played constructive roles. It has underpinned the creation of states that have established large zones of relative peace. Interpersonal violence has become unacceptable within most states, creating levels of personal security that would have been unthinkable for most of human history. Within these zones of peace, economies have flourished and many have lived longer lives than they might have otherwise. (Charles Tilly has argued that murder rates in modern England are about one-tenth of those of 800 years ago.[3])

But if it has sometimes helped reduce violence within modern states, nationalism has often failed to reduce violence between ethnic or national communities, while the organisational and technological ability to inflict violence has grown exponentially. In the era of nuclear weapons, the divisiveness of nationalist ideologies poses a danger to humanity as a whole and perhaps to the entire biosphere. It also makes it difficult to tackle the increasing number of problems that require global solutions, such as the threat of nuclear war or global warming, for politicians and voters who define themselves primarily as members of a particular nation will not find it easy to put global needs and priorities ahead of those of their own communities. Meanwhile, transnational organisations remain weak, in part because they, too, consist of individuals who think of themselves primarily as representatives of particular nations.

These dangers make it important to think hard about the possibility of creating a broader global identity that could co-exist with, but might occasionally override existing nationalisms; an ideology that could help humans see more easily what unites them rather than what divides them. In considering the possibilities for the emergence of some sort of global nationalism, the history of nationalism itself has much to teach us.

As modern states began to mobilise the human, economic and intellectual resources of their societies on unprecedented scales, they soon learned the power of nationalism as a force for cohesion. So it is not surprising that all modern states have actively sought to create and disseminate a sense of nationalism through national rituals and symbols, and through the way they educate the young. Historians played a vital role in constructing nationalist ideologies. From multiple, and sometimes contradictory stories about the past, they created new and larger imagined communities (in Benedict Anderson's phrase[4]), communities that could attract the loyalty of individuals from diverse backgrounds. Nationalist historians constructed new creation myths for each nation, tracing the essence of nationhood as far as they could in the past, and helping individuals to see themselves as part of something larger and more awesome than their families or their local communities.

But constructing such identities was never easy. Even in France, a country with more homogenous traditions than most, the task required a sustained educational effort; as Eugen Weber has shown, even in the late nineteenth century, many French citizens did not think of themselves first of all as French.[5] Gradually, however, the achievements of the historians such as Thomas Babington Macaulay, Vasilii Klyuchevskii and Manning Clarks were duplicated in country after country, and more and more people came to identify themselves passionately with the nations of which they were citizens. This complex and powerful intellectual achievement helps explain why history occupies so prominent a place in modern educational curricula.

If nationalist historiography could give diverse populations a sense of national unity, should it not be possible, in principle, to create even wider identities that embrace the entire world? At the 19th International Congress of Historical Sciences in Oslo, in August 2000, the archaeologist Andrew Sherratt invited the history profession to take up this challenge, to 'provide a more comprehensive vision which can appeal to human-kind in general, rather than simply to local segments of the world's population'.[6] The idea is not really new. H. G. Wells tried to write a universal history in the terrible aftermath of World War I. He concluded that traditional histories were bound to stir up endless warfare, and only a universal history could offer a way out of this deadly cycle.[7] Since Wells wrote, technological change, the multiplying environmental impacts of our species, and rapid globalisation have given the idea of a history of humanity increasing significance. These develop-ments have also made the idea more feasible, for it would have been difficult even to imagine a global community until very recently.

Few cultures prior to the European Enlightenment thought of the world as one whole and the people within it as a single generic humankind, above and beyond any sociological, bio-logical or spiritual distinctions. It is from within that discourse that we can describe a particular form of the globalisation of Culture, the emergence and diffusion of ideas and beliefs about the globe and humanity itself. Even though most people remain rooted in a local or national culture and a local place, it is becoming increasingly impossible for them to live in that place disconnected culturally from the world in which it is situated.[8]

Yet the task of constructing a global identity has turned out to be surprisingly difficult; indeed some have concluded that it can't be done. One problem is practical and institutional.

Emerging modern states had good reason to support the construction, the teaching and the propagation of nationalist ideologies. But they have little interest in the creation of even broader identities that might threaten or undermine national loyalties, and they have great power to limit the impact of ideologies they dislike. They control or influence school and college syllabi, they all enjoy significant leverage over the media, and in most societies they play a major role in maintaining the rituals of nationalism. There are, of course, forces and organisations that seek more global perspectives, including the many arms of the United Nations and non-governmental organisations such as the Red Cross or Amnesty International. But as yet, such organisations are far less powerful than the major nation states, and they can function efficiently only with the financial and political support of those states. I can see no simple way around this problem. If a powerful sense of global identity is to emerge, it will have to do so without the massive governmental support that helped create modern national identities.

This will not be easy. Even where states have joined together in larger structures, such as the European Union or the USSR, it is the national identities that have retained most power. In Europe, considerable resources have been devoted to the task of generating a sense of a common European identity, but according to polls in the early 1990s, fewer than 5 per cent of those interviewed thought of themselves primarily as Europeans, while 45 per cent claimed to have no sense at all of Europeanness. As David Held and his colleagues put it:

> if this is the best that can be managed after four decades of systematic effort in a region that possesses, for all its fault lines and geographical oddities, a sense of shared history and cultural inheritance and possesses transnational institutions of considerable political weight, how much harder will the task be at a transregional and global level?[9]

Other problems are political and conceptual. In *1984*, George Orwell imagined a world with just three huge empires that engaged in continuous warfare, not because they had any principled objections to each other's existence, but because having an enemy was such a powerful way of sustaining loyalty. Is it true, as Orwell implied, that a strong sense of shared identity cannot exist without warfare? If so, the idea of a sense of global identity is not worth pursuing. Cohesion at local or regional scales will always require conflict at larger scales, and a powerful sense of identity will always have to be forged on the anvil of national enmities. But is this necessarily true? Even if historians have tended to focus more on conflict than on co-operation in human history, co-operation and a sense of a common purpose have always been present, even between individuals who do not share human enemies. Merchants have co-operated over huge distances, even if their co-operation was always edged with rivalry. Families, kin groups, religious congregations, guilds and associations of many different kinds have co-operated on projects that did not necessarily entail the destruction of human rivals, and in the process, they have often generated or discovered a powerful sense of solidarity. So there is no fundamental reason to suppose that humans are incapable of co-operating without having a common enemy; abstract enemies such as global warming or the threat of nuclear war may be enough to generate a sense of shared purpose and shared community. Indeed, recent history contains several examples of global co-operation on disarmament and environmental issues such as the reduction in the use of chlorofluorocarbons (CFCs).

Anthony Smith has argued that the difficulties go even deeper, that the very idea of a 'global culture' is a 'practical impossibility, except in interplanetary terms. Even if the concept is predicated of *Homo sapiens*, as opposed to other species, the differences between segments of humanity in terms of lifestyle and belief-repertoire are too great, and the common elements too generalized, to permit us to even conceive of a globalized culture.'[10] However, Smith's own critique suggests the difficulties may not be as great as he suggests. Community identities, he argues, are based in subjective experiences arising from shared cultural and historical experiences. They imply a sense of continuity between generations, shared memories of specific events and a shared sense of destiny. And he concludes: 'It is in just these senses that "nations" can be understood as historic identities, or at least closely deriving from them, while a global and cosmopolitan culture fails to relate to any such historic identity. Unlike national cultures, a global culture is essentially memoryless.'[11] Yet is it not the job of historians to construct group memories, and is that not exactly what the great nationalist historians did? If they could construct vivid, evocative and powerful national stories from the extraordinarily diverse raw materials of nations such as the United States whose citizens came from all around the world, why should it be harder to do so for the wider community of humanity? Indeed, there are good reasons to suppose that constructing an identity that unites all humans ought to be a less artificial project than the construction of national identities, for the category of 'human being' can be defined with some precision in scientific terms, while national identities cannot.

I have argued that the construction of a sense of shared global identity between all humans is important; and I have also argued that the task will be difficult, but not impossible. But who will do it?

To the extent that the challenge is taken up by historians, it is most likely to be taken up by those who identify themselves as 'world' historians. Yet so far, few world historians have put the category of humanity at the centre of their work.[12] Most world historians are agreed that world history must escape the conceptual straitjacket of national historiography; in some sense, world history must be transnational. But what will this mean in practice? Since the publication of W. H. McNeill's immensely influential *Rise of the West* in 1963,[13] many world historians have concentrated on describing and comparing the histories of different 'civilizations' or culture regions, and many textbooks, today, still feel obliged to devote many chapters to the histories of particular civilisations. Yet McNeill himself had argued (and he made the point even more forcibly in later works) that what happened *between* civilisations might be even more important than what happened *within* them. In recent decades, many world historians have focused increasingly on intercivilisational or intercultural connections through trade, the exchange of religious and artistic ideas, or the swapping of technologies. Interregional studies encouraged world historians to describe networks of many different kinds, to look at diasporas of merchants or slaves, for example, or the spread of different crops between different world regions. The work of Immanuel Wallerstein highlighted the importance of what he called 'world-systems', large zones united mainly by commercial relations.[14] In the hands of other world historians, such as Janet Abu-Lughod or Andre Gunder Frank, the notion of world systems was broadened and shifted back in time. Agu-Lughod described a thirteenth-century world system, while Frank claimed to identify a trans-Eurasian system perhaps as long ago as 2000 BCE. More recently, Christopher Chase-Dunn and Thomas Hall have identified networks of communities linked by regional exchanges even in pre-state societies.[15]

All these approaches helped widen the lens through which historians viewed the past, but none really embraced the entire world as a unity. 'Global historians' have tried to do this, but have concluded that a unified history of the world can only be written for the modern era because only recently have new technologies of communications and transportation made it possible for particular effects to be felt throughout the world.

What is striking in all these approaches is the absence of the category of human beings. This is surprising because elsewhere the category has come into sharper focus as physical anthropologists have fleshed out the history of our species, and demonstrated our remarkable genetic homogeneity. There is now little disagreement about the fundamental coherence of the species. So here is a natural unifying category for world history. In principle, it ought to be possible to tell a historical story that is the story of all human beings, a story that tells of the trajectory of a single species, our own. If a global historical memory is to be created by world historians, it will surely have to take the category of human beings as its starting point. It will have to discuss how and when our species first emerged, what distinguishes us from other species, how our ancestors spread around the world during the Palaeolithic era, how they adapted to different environments, how agriculture appeared in many different parts of the world since the end of the last ice age, how human populations grew and became increasingly organised and efficient at extracting the resources they needed to support themselves, and finally how the modern world came into being in recent centuries.

Recently, the category of 'humanity' has begun to achieve more salience within world history. Jared Diamond's bestseller, *Guns, Germs and Steel*, looked at human history through the eyes of a biologist, for whom the species itself was the natural unit, and the central question he posed was why different populations of humans have had such different histories despite their unity as human beings.[16] William McNeill has also moved towards a more unified view of human history in his latest work, co-authored with his son, John McNeill. In *The Human Web*, the McNeills construct a history of humanity around a metaphor that gives priority to the links between human communities.[17] Within this conceptual framework, particular communities appear not as the basic units of human history but as products of something deeper. They are woven from the many skeins of culture, trade and descent that have linked human communities since the Paleolithic era. My own work has attempted to embed human history within the larger histories of the biosphere and the Universe as a whole, and within such a framework it is natural to think of human history as the history of a distinctive and highly original biological species.[18]

Gradually, world historians may be learning to see world history as the history of humanity. This suggests that the difficulties of creating a history of humanity that can inspire a sense of global identity will not be conceptual or even empirical; they will be institutional and artistic. The task is not impossible, merely difficult. The institutional difficulties will arise from the fact that world historians are unlikely to get the political and financial support that nationalist historians once enjoyed. The artistic difficulties arise from the fact that the biological category of humanity has a limited capacity to inspire loyalty. The challenge for the emerging community of world historians is to flesh out the story of humanity as nationalist historians once fleshed out the histories of particular nations, creating an authoritative, vivid and inspiring account that can appeal to all humans just because they are human. If world historians can assemble the story of humanity as successfully as nationalist historians assembled the stories of particular nations, they may contribute something of profound importance to the future of our species.

NOTES

[1]   Alexander McCall Smith, *The No. 1 Ladies' Detective Agency*, Anchor Books, New York, 2002 (first published 1998), p. 35.

[2]   Ross Poole, *Nations and Identity*, Routledge, London and New York, 1999, pp. 15–16.

[3]   Charles Tilly, *Coercion, Capital, and European States, AD 990–1992*, Blackwell, Cambridge, Mass., 1992, p. 69.

[4]   Benedict Anderson, *Imagined Communities*, rev. edn, Verso, London and New York, 1991.

[5]   Eugen Weber, *Peasants into Frenchmen: The Modernization of Rural France, 1870–1914*, Stanford University Press, Stanford, CA, 1976.

[6]   Andrew Sherratt, 'Archaeology and World History', *International Congress of Historical Sciences*, Nasjonalbiblioteket, Oslo, 2000, p. 23.

7   H. G. Wells, *An Outline of History: Being a Plain History of Life and Mankind*, 7th revision, Cassell and Co., London, 1932, pp. 1–2.

8   David Held, Anthony McGrew, David Goldblatt and Jonathan Perraton, *Global Transformations: Politics, Economics and Culture*, Polity Press, Cambridge, 1999, p. 339.

9   Held et al., *Global Transformations*, p. 375.

10 Cited in Held et al., *Global Transformations*, p. 239.

11 Held et al., *Global Transformations*, p. 241.

12 For two recent discussions of the current state of world history, see Ross E. Dunn, *The New World History: A Teacher's Companion* (Bedford, Boston and New York, 2000) and Patrick Manning, *Navigating World History: Historians Create a Global Past* (Palgrave Macmillan, New York, 2003).

13 William H. McNeill, *The Rise of the West: A History of the Human Community*, University of Chicago Press, Chicago, 1963; reprinted 1991, with a retrospective essay, 'The rise of the West after twenty-five years'.

14 Immanuel Wallerstein, *The Modern World-System I: Capitalist Agriculture and the Origins of the European World-Economy in the Sixteenth Century*, Academic Press, New York, 1974; on Wallerstein's impact on world history, see the brief discussion in Patrick Manning, *Navigating World History*, pp. 61–5.

15 Janet Abu-Lughod, *Before European Hegemony: The World System AD 1250–1350*, Oxford University Press, New York, 1989; A. G. Frank and Barry K. Gills (eds), *The World System: From Five Hundred Years to Five Thousand*, Routledge, London and New York, 1992; Christopher Chase-Dunn and Thomas D. Hall, *Rise and Demise: Comparing World Systems*, Westview Press, Boulder, CO, 1997.

16 Jared Diamond, *Guns, Germs and Steel*, Vintage, London, 1998.

17 J. R. McNeill and William H. McNeill, *The Human Web: A Bird's-Eye View of World History*, W. W. Norton, New York and London, 2003.

18 David Christian, *Maps of Time: An Introduction to Big History*, University of California Press, Berkeley, CA, 2004; David Christian, 'World history in context', *Journal of World History*, vol. 14, no. 4, 2003, pp. 437–58.

CHAPTER 13

IAIN McCALMAN

FLIRTING WITH FICTION

One of the unexpected casualties of our current History Wars may be a forced cooling of relations between fiction and history writing, disciplines whose creative interchanges have illuminated western intellectual life for the past forty years. I'm sad about this, even as I proclaim it. As long as I can remember, I've loved historical fiction and treated it as inspiration for my history studies. Growing up remote from libraries and bookshops in Central Africa, I was intoxicated by the swash-buckling tales of historical adventure and romance that I found on my parents' bookshelves, and I blame the enticements of historical novels like Stevenson's *Kidnapped* and Scott's *Ivanhoe* for my gravitation to studying the cultural history of British Romanticism.

Not surprisingly I was also one of those historians attracted to literary and critical theory at a time, during the 1970s and 1980s, when intellectuals of every stripe were struggling to come to grips with the implications of the so-called 'linguistic turn'. The contention that language creates rather than reflects meaning had seismic implications for historical practice. If this was so, how could we find the bedrock of reality outside the text? It followed that all social, political and economic life should to be treated as textual, and that history–writing was really a branch of poetics or aesthetics. For some of us, this was an exhilarating discovery, for others it represented a dangerous retreat from the authority that the discipline of history had painstakingly accumulated as an empirical social science. In its extreme formulation, the linguistic turn seemed to elide the distinction between fiction and history altogether—at the very least it blurred the line between our products and those of good historical novelists such as Iain Pears, Susan Sontag and Barry Unsworth.

Responding to this challenge, two of America's most distinguished historiographers, Hayden White and Dominic LaCapra, urged us in a series of influential studies to throw off social scientific pretensions and embrace our affinities with literature and art. White argued that most academic historians were unaware of the fact that they actually shaped their analyses according to a series of foundational literary plots and tropes.[1] LaCapra was more troubled about the unimaginative way in which we made these literary borrowings. Our favourite model seemed to be the nineteenth-century realist novel. This in turn tended to produce a chronological historical narrative written from the perspective of a single omniscient narrator. LaCapra contended that such a dull and routine product represented a dereliction of our duty as creative writers, and it helped to explain the limitations of our social influence. Where, he asked, were the contested voices, the multiple viewpoints, the raids on the unconscious, the Rabelaisian dialogues that had been pioneered by modernist novelists like Joyce or Faulkner? A century of narrative experimentation within the world of fiction had somehow passed us by.[2]

Impulses to merge history and fiction came equally strongly from the literary world. In the insatiable quest for new plots and structures, late twentieth-century western novelists have increasingly mimicked the language, methods, and materials of historians. It's not unusual these days for novels to reproduce realistic-looking fake documents in their texts, and some will go to the lengths of inventing an entire research apparatus of footnotes, references and bibliography. It's standard practice, too, for novelists to rely on historical research for parts of their narrative, then move seamlessly into imagined history without leaving behind any markers. And why should they? This cross fertilisation between fiction and history has given rise to the burgeoning new genre of 'historical faction', complete with its own canon and conventions. At the Canberra Press Club recently, Peter Carey grew understandably testy with journalists who criticised his *True History of the Kelly Gang* (2000) on the grounds that his mythic inventions might supplant the real-life accounts of historians. Too bad, was his rejoinder, that was the historians' problem; as a novelist, he could say what he liked. And of course he is right. Whether historical novelists are scrupulous or cavalier with historical evidence is irrelevant because their work proclaims itself to the world as imagined. The most one can ask is that it conveys a feeling of authentic history, and that is solely an aesthetic judgement.

More troubling for historians is a growing trend among some fiction writers to preface their books with the claim, 'based on authentic historical research'. The implication, of course, is that the work should be taken seriously as history. The writers are thereby asking to have their cake and eat it. They can benefit from the 'truth' status of history without being subject to the stringent tests of evidence that historians must expect. Whether their research is thin, slanted or naively positivist, it declares itself as fact. Sixty years of debate within our profession about the epistemological and ontological status of the historical fact is utterly irrelevant. Who among their readers either knows or cares?

Dan Brown's galloping bestseller, *The Da Vinci Code* (2003), is a case in point. It's a wooden and derivative who-dunnit that gains its power entirely from the sensational historical claims it purports to reveal. The book tells the story of an ancient conspiracy on the part of the Christian Church to suppress its true origins as a sacred feminine cult based on the worship of Mary Magdalene. Mary, it seems, was not a prostitute but Jesus Christ's wife and the founder of the Merovingian line of monarchs in France. This sensational truth has been preserved since the eleventh century by a real-life secret society based in France, called the Priory of Sion. The Roman Catholic Church, in particular, must stop at nothing to prevent disclosure of the secret.

This is intriguing background material for a thriller, albeit borrowed from an earlier 'non-fiction' bestseller about Mary Magdalene and the holy grail, but as history it's so shonky we wouldn't expect anyone to take it seriously. Dan Brown, though, is deadly serious. A preamble to the novel under the heading, 'Fact', asserts the centuries-old existence of the Priory of Sion and declares that 'all descriptions . . . of secret rituals in this novel are accurate'. A few conscientious reviewers who've bothered to check these claims have listed scores of historical howlers, including the fact that the Priory of Sion is actually an obscure and flaky occult society founded in Paris during World War II by a right-wing collaborator.

Make no mistake, it's Dan Brown's history rather than the clunky plot that has attracted buyers in droves—more than six million of them so far. Popular debate about the book centres almost exclusively on the accuracy of his anti-Catholic conspiracy. More surprising is the fact that most reviewers in the United States have taken Brown's historical claims at face value. Some even gush about his 'impeccable research'. In effect, the trappings of a thriller are allowed to serve as a Trojan Horse for bogus history. And there's no doubting that Brown has struck a populist chord. Judging from the massive internet correspondence, his thesis appeals particularly to those who want to see Christianity as a misogynist conspiracy, or to anti-Catholics who are thrilled at the implied connection of the Vatican with murder and corruption, or to those who cannot resist conspiracy theories of any kind. Dan Brown, meantime, remains impervious to criticism: when challenged, he can simply whip on the fig-leaf of 'fiction' to cover his historical nakedness.

Why should historians care that bestselling novelists get away with writing dubious history? The short answer is that unless we distinguish ourselves from false practitioners, we're in danger of being discredited with them. In museums, in the media, in the courts and in universities, professional historians are being required as never before to defend the truth value of our discipline. We must face the brutal reality that it is the public and the government, rather than our own academic peers, whom we must persuade of our social and intellectual worth and who, directly or indirectly, pay for our research. Part of what is at stake in the History Wars is how we are able to assert and defend our authority as expert professionals whose methods can be tested and replicated no less than those of social and natural scientists.

For this reason today's historians need to be acutely conscious of the dangers of using fiction in such a way as to blur the lines between our different practices. Recently I was offered the chance to write a 'trade' history aimed at a general reading market. I grabbed it because I've always hankered for an audience beyond the academy, even though I realised that it would mean making changes to my usual modes of writing and thinking. I was aware that my key shift would be from using the analytical models of the social sciences to using the narrative approaches of literature. Though narrative is unfashionable in professional history circles, it's the dominant mode of the popular market, and I wanted to give it a go. I also felt that a narrative approach might enable me to bring my literary and historical interests into closer convergence.

I was contracted to tell the story of an infamous European charlatan, freemason, alchemist and healer of the late eighteenth century, and my proposed title was *The Seven Ordeals of Count Cagliostro*. I hoped in writing the book to meld the insights and research methods of a professional historian with the plot structures and narrative techniques of a fiction writer. It proved easier said than done. On submitting a swag of draft chapters to my editor in the United States, I was chastened to have him write back: 'Now for the eighth ordeal of Iain McCalman—to turn an interesting study into a fast-paced story.' But I also discovered to my surprise that he was not at all interested in modernist or postmodernist narrative models. On the contrary, I was urged to go back to basics. He suggested that I needed, first, to construct a time-line and follow it scrupulously so as to prevent confusion in the minds of my readers. Second, I must at all costs avoid casting doubt on the veracity of my sources because it would damage my reader's 'necessary suspension of disbelief'. Finally, I was asked to make my depiction of Cagliostro's character less ambiguous. Readers would not want to be left in a state of uncertainty as to whether my protagonist was a saint or sinner; I had to tell them decisively one way or the other. Forget all the hard-won lessons of the linguistic turn. Forget moral ambiguity, contested voices, multiple perspectives, elusive meanings and surreal conjunctions: as far as the mass market was concerned: the model of the nineteenth-century realist novel must be the summit of my aspiration.

To be fair, we eventually struck a compromise. I worked to clarify the chronology, and my editor approved a reasonably experimental narrative structure. I presented Count Cagliostro through the eyes of seven major historical contemporaries, each of whom encountered him very differently. Indirectly, each of these seven narrators drew attention to the subjectivity of their viewpoint and their sources. Readers had to make their own critical evaluations of the historical witnesses. Even the ambiguity surrounding my personal judgement of Cagliostro was allowed to pass. Readers were permitted to make up their own minds on the basis of the conflicting evidence presented. To my surprise, also, no attempt was made to curtail my reference apparatus. Footnotes were fine as long as they

were discreetly hidden at the end of the book and not signalled in the text. That way, ordinary readers could act as if the
references didn't exist, and scholars or pedants could turn
quietly to the back to check the evidence.

Rather more disturbing, however, was my gradual realisation that the press didn't share my perverse insistence on the
distinction between history and fiction. It was unsettling
enough to have my editor refer to the book as 'your novel', but
I was shocked when he suggested plot enhancements without
any historical warrant or urged me to alter the words in quotations because they might offend the puritanical sensibilities
of American general readers. I had to insist, for example, that
when a Roman Inquisitor reported in 1789 that Count Cagliostro had ridiculed Catholicism by pointing his finger up his
'arse', that we were not entitled in the interests of delicacy to
change the word to 'derriere'. But this cavalier attitude to evidence was, I found, pretty endemic to the whole world of the
US trade press, extending from editors, through marketeers,
public relations experts and cover designers. While the book
was to be sold as 'non fiction', this was not be taken too liter-
ally; it was simply the label for a market niche.

Newspaper reviews brought a fresh set of surprises on this
score. I was, of course, delighted to have the Oxford literary
scholar Peter Conrad say that the book had 'the teasing,
exciting psychological ambiguity of the best fiction',[3] and I
felt vindicated when several reviewers recognised that I'd
mimicked the eighteenth-century literary form of the pic-
aresque by chronicling the adventures of a travelling rogue. I
enjoyed reviewers recommending the book as a 'page turner',
and I didn't even mind it being called 'an eighteenth-century
road movie' or 'a ripping historical yarn'.[4] I'd not bargained,
though, on having one reviewer describe the book as 'a mix of
fiction and history', or on being criticised by another for
inventing Cagliostro's conversations.[5] She assumed that there
was no possibility of eighteenth-century dialogue having been
recorded in contemporary documents. Of course, she might

have checked at the back of the book and found the references to court records and inquisition interrogations. Then again, why should she? My endnotes were so coyly concealed that it was perfectly natural to overlook them. In this sense, I had only myself to blame. At the very least, I should have included one of those statements at the beginning of the book saying that all dialogue came from original sources. This is the type of thing an academic takes for granted, forgetting that a mass-market publisher feels no responsibility or incentive to patrol the borderline between historical truth and fantasy.

I can't really complain about being misinterpreted. If one feasts with panthers, one must expect the odd scratch. We can hardly blame commercial press editors and fiction writers for erasing the borders between fiction and history when we fail to draw a line in the sand ourselves. My book on Cagliostro is, I believe, a history. It is as intensively researched as any of my more explicitly academic studies. My descriptions, say, of Queen Marie-Antoinette's emotional state after the acquittal of her enemy Cardinal Rohan in 1785, or of the brutal weather in Bienne (Switzerland) on a particular day in 1788, come not solely from my imagination but from having sifted through reams of letters and manuscripts which reveal these points. I've not knowingly made up anything that isn't in the historical records—partial, subjective and ambiguous though these are. Of course the book is my subjective interpretation of Cagliostro. I don't pretend to tell *the* historical truth about this enigmatic man, no one can ever do that; but my book is always constrained by the surviving historical sources and by a repertoire of well-tested methods of assessing evidence, how-ever poorly or skilfully these might have been practised. Still, if I have connived in allowing the book to *seem* like a fiction to the extent that readers and reviewers become confused, then I must stand condemned.

I'm not suggesting for a moment that historians should stop writing books that experiment with fictional techniques

or publishing articles that celebrate the epistemological kin-
ship between history and fiction. I have no doubt whatsoever
that history is a form of poetics. But one of the casualties of
our 'History Wars' is, I fear, the necessity for historians to signal
their experiments with fiction with exaggerated care. We cannot afford to leave hostages for those who want to diminish
the truth value of our discipline. The lesson of the historians
of the Jewish Holocaust is a grim reminder of this. When in
the future we historians flirt with the models and styles of
fiction, we need at the same time to make clear that our two
enterprises remain separated by the one simple and unbridge-
able distinction that historians cannot make up their facts
(however elusive the status of a fact might be). Otherwise,
readers, reviewers and government officials will end up treating our work as invention, and our ability to influence the
world will be that much diminished. In the interests of avant-
garde experimentation, the Princeton historian Simon Schama
is perfectly within his rights to juxtapose real and imagined
histories in his book *Dead Certainties* (1991),[6] and the English
biographer Peter Ackroyd is equally entitled in his life of
Charles Dickens to insert passages of imaginary conversation
with literary figures like Chatterton, Wilde and T. S. Eliot.[7] But
if historians want to play these games, we must trumpet to our
readers when and where we have crossed over into fantasy.

I recently saw a stimulating TV biography of George Orwell
made by the independent British producer Alex Graham and
his imaginative team at Wall-to-Wall. No contemporary television company has been more enterprising in imparting a
fresh fizz to the historical documentary. They are prepared to
combine traditional film documentary and innovative re-
enactment techniques in a brilliantly innovatory mix, and
they're not afraid to use contemporary pop images and songs,
or to blend realist and surreal imagery. The new documentary
of Orwell pushes this experimentation a step further. In one
scene, Orwell, who is represented by an actor with an uncanny

physical resemblance, ruminates in the trenches during the Spanish Civil War of 1936–37. A grainy, flickering, black-and-white newsreel achieves a stunning impression of authenticity. But it is all invented. Elsewhere, too, Orwell's fictional conversations are interlaced with genuine documentary footage. One needs to be an Orwell expert to detect the simulations. Perhaps Orwell himself would not have minded this sleight of hand: his own gritty social documentaries of the 1930s are said to be some of the earliest examples of modern literary 'faction'. Moreover, Alex Graham's analysis of Orwell undoubtedly contains great 'poetic truth': it is perceptive, informed and original. So why complain?

Complain we must; because, however imaginative they might be, works like these are committing a form of historical fraud. Ultimately they will depreciate the commodity of history itself. However curmudgeonly and boring it makes us look, we cannot allow them to pass as history because they are inventions posing as histories. W. H. Auden is said to have exulted in the fact that 'poetry changes nothing': maybe so, but I submit that this is not an appropriate slogan for the historian. History can and should change things; and we must protect that right and ability to our last breath.

NOTES

[1] Hayden White, *Tropics of Discourse: Essays in Cultural Criticism*, John Hopkins University Press, Baltimore, 1978; *The Content of the Form: Narrative Discourse and Historical Representation*, Johns Hopkins University Press, Baltimore, 1987.

[2] Dominick LaCapra, *Rethinking Intellectual History: Texts, Contexts, Language*, Cornell University Press, Ithaca, New York, 1983.

[3] Cited in Iain McCalman, *The Last Alchemist: Count Cagliostro, Master of Magic in the Age of Reason*, Harper Collins, New York, 2003.

[4] Bill Saunders, 'The charlatan's art', *The Independent on Sunday*, 13 July 2003; John Rickard, 'The crook with a great soul',

   Australian Review of Books, June–July 2003; Brenda Niall, *The Age
   Review*, 26 July 2003.
5 Glenda Guest, *Muse,* September 2003.
6 Simon Schama, *Dead Certainties: Unwarranted Speculations*, Knopf,
   New York, 1991.
7 Peter Ackroyd, *Dickens*, Sinclair Stevenson, London, 1990,
   pp. 450–5.

INDEX